THE PAUL FACTOR

FORREST DAVIS

authorHOUSE®

AuthorHouse™ LLC
1663 Liberty Drive
Bloomington, IN 47403
www.authorhouse.com
Phone: 1-800-839-8640

Published by AuthorHouse   06/12/2014

ISBN: 978-1-4969-1580-1 (sc)
ISBN: 978-1-4969-1581-8 (e)

Library of Congress Control Number: 2014909757

Being supported
by scripture, what
is written here
challenges a significant
portion of Christian
doctrine that has
been promoted and
practiced for almost
2,000 years. Generally
speaking, people are
reluctant to change
their many differing
Christian concepts
even though they may
have no biblical basis
for many things they
have been taught.
Consequently and
unfortunately, most
are uncomfortable
talking about what
they believe and it is
seldom discussed.....
by anyone.

"Let us hear the conclusion of the whole matter: Fear God and keep his commandments; for this is the whole duty of man." (Eccl. 12:13)

"Wherewith shall I come before the LORD, and bow myself before the high God? Shall I come before him with burnt offerings, with calves of a year old? Will the LORD be pleased with thousands of rams, or with ten thousands of rivers of oil? Shall I give my firstborn for my transgression, the fruit of my body for the sin of my soul? He hath showed you, O man, what is good; and what doth the LORD require of thee, but to do justly, and to love mercy, and to walk humbly with thy God?" (Mica 6:6-8)

Paul, a self-appointed "Apostle," redefined Christianity while ignoring these scriptures and other significant doctrine coming from the Old Testament. This is primarily what Jesus said He came to teach. Jesus' message was simple and although Paul changed many things Jesus taught and made His simple message complicated, "organized" Christianity has given priority to what Paul taught while ignoring Jesus.

TABLE OF CONTENTS

ABOUT THE AUTHOR

Forrest Davis was born on April 30, 1928 in Weatherford, Texas.

He was raised in a traditional Southern Baptist family who were very active in attending and supporting their local Church. Some of his diversified accomplishments include licensed pilot, computer technician in the 50's, certified member "American Society of Traffic & Transportation," railroad director, executive in a large international company, active US Naval Air Reserve, and Christmas tree farmer. His hobbies include art, photography, cartooning, music, softball, golf, fishing, writing, and reading.

Davis has authored three other books critiquing Christianity as it is taught and practiced: A View From The Pew, Let Us Create God In Our Own Image, and Ole Wives Tales and Church Doctrine. His books reflect an evolution of opinion over a ten year period on such subjects as the trinity as well as the definition of just who Jesus was and the stated purpose of His mission. Over time, the studies that went into writing those first three books led him to an inescapable conclusion: Paul changed significant teachings of Jesus and even reversed Jesus' instructions. This had the affect of putting men in charge of institutional Christianity and subsequently in charge of those seeking God through Jesus.

THE ISSUE

It is said that a person can become very unpopular by messing around with other peoples' religion. I understand full well it could be like inviting hell-fire and brimstone to come raining down on one's head. I am also aware that by doing so a person could achieve (among Christian brethren) the reputation of being a "religious nut," "a scripture lawyer," "a KJV bible thumper," or perhaps even the dreaded "hypocrite."

There's obviously no gain to me personally by venturing into such an endeavor. Who in their right mind would actually attempt swimming up Niagara Falls? It would be like forcing your way onto the playing field in the super bowl game and insisting on becoming the quarterback for both teams. I just believe, in this case, the research I have done is interesting enough to record and there are others who will also find it interesting. What! You're actually going to do it? What a "dumb-ass!" (Taken from the Biblical expression in 2nd Pet. 2:16…. You gotta go to KJV to get the good stuff).

Actually, what's really going on here is the questioning of what I myself was taught about Christianity as compared to writings in the Bible. Most of what I have written is verifiable history which will stand to anyone's research. It's really a neat study and there's not one sermon to be found; opinions… yes, sermons… no way. (That is almost true)

<u>And now the issue</u>: There is a "Paul Factor" cloud that hovers over the New Testament that deserves at least a conversation. Paul's "conversion" to Christianity occurred 37 years after Jesus' death and resurrection and although Paul never met Jesus in person, he nevertheless went on to personally define Jesus and Christianity for most of the Christian world. On one occasion Paul "made no bones" about what he perceived to be his authority. According to him, he was given absolute and total latitude to carry out a mission that apparently <u>he himself</u> defined when he stated in Col. 1:25:

> *"I am made a minister, according to the dispensation of God which is given to me for you, to fulfill the word of God."*

The wording of that authority has no resemblance to the authority also said to be given to Paul by Jesus' Spirit on the road to Damascus. The following is what Paul said Jesus initially told him:

> *"To open their eyes, and to turn them from darkness to light, and from the power of Satan unto God, that they may receive forgiveness of sins.* (Acts 26:18)"

If those were the instructions actually given by Jesus, then that is the only authority Paul had and it was very specifically (and only) intended to bring repentance to the Gentiles by teaching them to love God and to love others. Even though

Paul went on to correctly teach many things about God and His word, he also took it on himself to… (As he would then later describe it) "FULFILL" that word. However, when he "fulfilled" it, he generously changed some of it, then added to it and then took away from it. Since Paul assumed to have such authority, whatever he decided to teach was to be the fulfillment of the word. Ultimately, that "fulfillment" would give his perception of spirituality priority over the written word and eventually (in today's culture) came to discount most of it altogether.

It wasn't that Paul had a different teaching style than Jesus. It wasn't that Paul added teachings here and there that expanded or complimented the principle messages that Jesus taught. Paul, in fact, contradicted Jesus on significant issues that define Christianity and planted those seeds of contradiction in a garden of truth, mixing them with the "good seed" already planted there.

The condition was first called to my attention many years ago by my Brother-in-law and good friend, the late Dr. Grady Etheridge. Grady conducted a worldwide Bible teaching television program named "School of the Bible" on station TCT in Marion Illinois. While not addressing the details, Grady said to me several times: "Have you ever wondered why The Apostle Paul taught so differently than Jesus?" At that time I didn't know enough about the issues to discuss them but I never forgot his remarks. I'm not insinuating here that Grady would have endorsed any of my conclusions in this writing. I, of course don't know what position he would

5

have taken on the specific subjects I have summarized, but I suspect that he would have been reluctant to agree with some of them. On the other hand, Grady was open to genuine honest debate and I have seen him change his mind about things that he once believed.

In recent years, being reminded of what Grady had said, I began to compare what Paul taught with what Jesus taught and as I compared their teachings, I began to ponder the question: "How is it possible that such a large part of the Christian community ignores what Jesus taught and follows after Paul even when some of Paul's teachings are totally opposite to Jesus' teachings?" What I finally discovered about Paul represents the culmination of an evolutionary journey I took studying scripture and Christian history over a period of six or seven years. The process of those studies eventually pointed to the Apostle Paul and his writings as being the catalyst that brought about the redefinition of the original Jesus-based Christianity. When the spot lights began to turn on one at a time, there stood Paul in the middle of the stage with all the lights pointing directly at him. That revelation about Paul changed many significant things I was once led to believe.

I eventually came to realize that Grady's observation of Paul's' writings are not a new revelation by any means. All the way back to the beginning of Paul's ministry, those remaining loyal to the beliefs of Jesus disciples were alienated from Paul and the doctrines he introduced into Christianity which were applied to Jesus whom they had known. The apostles Peter and

James were clearly thought of by Paul as being his adversaries (Gal. 2:11). Even Barnabas, Paul's bosom buddy, abandoned him. There have since been many scholars who also took issue with some of Paul's doctrines but the institutional churches are too deeply committed to the gospel of Paul to consider them seriously. Those folks that endorse Paul's doctrines will likely admit (if they are honest with themselves) that the teachings of Paul are more about Paul than about Jesus.

This writing goes further to document that most elements of mainstream Christian doctrine come from Paul and not from Jesus.

It's time to take a deep breath and attempt to add some logical perspective to the whole issue that is being discussed here. Just why did Paul teach so many things that wonderfully lined-up with the teachings of God and Jesus and then also teach contradiction to them as well as create new doctrines having nothing to do with what God and Jesus had taught? It is possible that with all the re-juggling of scripture by political "holy men," these contradictory positions could have been added to Paul's original writings in order to establish their credibility (as having come from Paul). None of that can be proven however and since it is labeled as being Paul's writings, we have to treat it as such. That's just the way it is and it doesn't alter the fact that we must confront obvious contradictions with what Jesus taught. It is interesting that the conflicts within Paul's teachings have been widely discussed within the theological community for almost 2000 years, yet have still been allowed to stand and with all due respect to Jesus, they cannot continue to be ignored.

That being said, Paul is the only person that ever used the word "dispensation" in his writings and I believe he deliberately chose that particular word knowing full well he was into creating a new religious order using the framework of God/Jehovah as its origin. It was to be a new order that he would also attach to the name "Jesus" while ignoring key things that Jesus taught. Even though he may have thought he had the authority and was on solid ground, that doesn't make it so. Read on.

The Gospel according to Paul (All of Paul's combined writings) is unique and different compared to any other gospel and over the years became the foundation for church institutions as they defined and promoted Christianity. Most of what Paul wrote written between 50 and 67 AD had anything to do with other gospels from those people who actually lived and traveled with Jesus because none of that was yet written; it rather was reported by Paul to have come to him from Jesus' Spirit. This study challenges that portion of what Paul taught that contradicts Jesus' teachings as reported in the four gospels of Matthew, Mark, Luke and John. There are a number of conflicting differences and since they are not both correct, we are at times forced by scripture to choose between Paul and Jesus. We cannot have it both ways when they disagree and we cannot choose one while ignoring the other. In fact, we must go with one and discount the other. Remarkably, even after reading the differences in scripture, many will continue to follow Paul. I will go with Jesus.

I don't believe anyone ever talks about such things because we're so overcome by the aura of Godliness and the majesty of the priesthood with their bible seminaries and their Doctor Degrees and their Godly claims and their five hundred million dollar "worship center" palaces, we are afraid to utter one word of dissent for fear of being branded either stupid or a trouble-maker. The Bible tells us to "seek and ye shall find," yet, for the most part, they would not allow us to seek anything. We are more or less expected to sit down and shut-up and be nice to each other. So, following their simple rules we became programmed in such a way that when we read obvious conflicting statements in the Bible we don't even acknowledge to ourselves they exist. I will illustrate some of them which are truly surprising. Just read them for yourself; and yes, they were meant to be read as they were initially written.

When we went to them searching for God, the programs they directed at us were professionally staged productions aligned with today's culture. From the congregation came chants like "Thank you Jesus," "We love you Jesus," "You are worthy Jesus" and then they started patting us on the back and hugging on us and grinning (not making fun of chanting or patting or hugging or grinning). They were so sweet and kind we didn't want to hurt their feelings by questioning anything they taught; besides that, most everybody likes to be hugged on, including me. Even without the hugging, I still could not have resisted the grinning. I would have automatically grinned back and then I would have been trapped. Seriously, because of those things we are willing to let them dictate the terms of our life with no questions asked. We went there and sat with them as if around the warmth of their campfire and stared mesmerized into its flames as we all sang love songs to Jesus in hushed tones and became captured by their gift to us of God; then they went on to teach us mostly about how to become followers of the "Apostle" Paul, rather than followers of Jesus. Say what? Yes! They stamped "Jesus" on our foreheads and then dressed us up in a "Paul" uniform.

The Apostle Paul is quoted by Protestant Church Institutions more than any other personality in the Bible, including the teachings from God the Father through the prophets as well as from Jesus through His Apostles. In fact, Paul's doctrines are the backbone of many institutionalized Churches; and as it turns out, it was Paul's personal opinions, rather than Jesus', that came to define some of the major components of Christianity as it is taught and practiced. As Paul defined Christianity in what now comprises a large part of the New Testament, he actually changed some of the basic fundamentals that God and Jesus had established as well as made-up some of his own and many Christian Institutions endorse his teachings on basic subjects like: The definition of Christianity, Church, Prayer, Salvation, Righteousness, God's grace, The Holy Spirit and others.

Paul complicated Jesus' simple messages when he attempted to define and interject the Spiritual aspects of it all. There is no question that Christianity's' definition and practice of spiritual matters are more influenced by Paul than by Jesus Himself. With Matthew, Mark, Luke and John, it was all about the "Word" that came from God's Spirit through the prophets as well as from Jesus' teachings. With Paul it appears to be more about his perception of spiritual matters based on what he believed to be those personal encounters with Jesus' Spirit. So, from Matthew, Mark, Luke and John it was from Jesus' lips. From Paul it was from Jesus' Spirit. After reading it all, one may conclude that in order to believe some of the things Paul taught we would have to deny the eye witness reports from all four of Jesus' companion-Apostles.

It was Paul's personal definition of spirituality that created the very foundation of Christian doctrine that has been practiced by many. That conclusion does not deny that spirituality also has a significant role in a Jesus-based Christian philosophy; however, the two teachings are quite different. When Paul created and installed his perceived elements of "worship," he treated The Holy Spirit almost as if it had emerged a new Spirit from Jesus at His death and resurrection; yet, according to Jesus it was the Spirit of God that God the Father was to send to comfort us. It was to be God's Spirit sent on Jesus' behalf to those that believed and it was to be sent by God Himself (John 14:26).

Paul taught the opposite to Jesus when he said in Gal. 4:6 *"And because ye are sons, God hath sent forth the Spirit of his Son into your hearts, crying, Abba, Father."* Paul also taught in Romans 8:26-34 that our access to God is filtered through an intercession to God by Jesus Spirit. Although Jesus taught that God the Father would send His Spirit to guide us in the truth of scripture (John 14:23-26), Paul taught that God put Jesus' Spirit in our hearts to be an intermediary between God and mankind.

The Spirit of God the Father either directly visits man's spirit or He doesn't. Although Paul endorsed both positions; for the most part he would lead us to Jesus' Spirit and away from God the Father's Spirit…. away from that Old Testament toward what Paul termed the "New dispensation" that he himself designed. Our having direct access to God the Father does not diminish Jesus' role in that relationship. Scripture clarified that many times in the four gospels as Jesus explained the relationship between God the Father, Himself and mankind (John 17th chapter).

Paul's multiple-choice "now you see it-now you don't" version of spirituality often collided with the authority of the rest of the bible and Paul's teachings effectively changed Jesus' teachings about the relationship between mankind, God the Father and Himself. I suspect that Paul's conflicting teachings were at least partly responsible for the creation of the "Trinity" doctrine. The Trinity concept combined God the Father, The Holy Spirit/Ghost and Jesus into a single entity. It was invented by "church-handlers" about 400 years after Jesus' death and resurrection and it helped smooth-over many unexplainable and conflicting statements in scripture, particularly those made by Paul. As an example, Paul had independently declared in Col. 1:15 that Jesus *"is the image of the invisible God"* and that statement is reconciled only by use of the "Trinity" doctrine. Paul's conflicting writings may also be credited with the origin of the so-called "Rapture" doctrine which was discovered and/or invented about 1700 years after Jesus' death. Neither of those strange doctrines would have been invented just to make Paul's writings fit in with the rest of the bible because they are not found in the rest of the bible except through innuendo (just as with Paul's writings). They were likely invented in order to pull together Paul's many disconnected statements and they did all of that just to be able to endorse Paul's definition of Spirituality and the particular way he applied it to the "Church" as well as to the practice of Christianity. Reconciling Paul's conflicting statements insured the institution's authority and control over the church and most all of the changes were brought about by the institution itself. We "sheep" have always done just what we were told to do.

Based on Paul's writings about the spiritual nature of Christianity, it is conceivable that he also had direct input in the writing of the Book of Acts. I, of course, have no proof of that. On the other hand, there was more written detail about Paul in the Book of Acts than of any other person and if it looks like a duck....it could be a duck. Two thirds of the entire book is written about Paul and contains detailed accounts of many of his personal conversations with many different people, as well as details of his travels over a period of several years. Also, there appears to be just too much written there about Paul's version of spirituality for anyone else to have written it. For starters it highlights Paul's "New Dispensation" as having become a substitute for what Jesus had taught about repentance. In Acts 19:1-10, Paul is quoted as giving a person's <u>receiving</u> of the "Holy Ghost" priority over what Jesus' taught about repenting and pursuing God's righteousness. There, he made negative reference to John the Baptist's "baptism of repentance" while ignoring that Jesus had also taught repentance. The teaching and application of being "baptized in the Spirit" (as some practice it) originated with Paul and Paul alone.

As it turns out, the book of "Acts" provided the foundation and authority for Paul's work going forward. First of all, it put Paul on relatively equal footing with the 12 Apostles that Jesus had already appointed. Although some have designated the Apostle Luke as being the author of the book, it is also possible that Paul either wrote it or at least shared its authorship. Being written somewhat different than Paul's "letters," he would have written it to be a foundational documentary rather than in the same style as his typical letters of instruction to newly planted churches.

As we begin this study we can first remind ourselves that Paul was not "The Christ" ….. "The Messiah;"…..that of course was Jesus and it was Jesus that was given God's authority, not Paul as Paul stated in Col. 1:25. I have read all of Paul's writings many times and I love and admire the way he emphasized many of the fundamentals that Jesus taught as well as his unyielding commitment to a mission that eventually led to his martyrdom (according to church custom). He was by far the most creative writer in the New Testament. The 13th chapter of 1st Corinthians is one of my favorite writings in all of scripture and is wonderfully expressed. It is hard to understand how Paul could have written such a thing while on other occasions teaching the opposite of what Jesus taught. One has to ask themselves: "Could all of these writings assigned to Paul actually be what he originally wrote?" That question cannot be answered and we can only deal with what's before us.

It is difficult to critique Paul in the manner I have done here because I fully appreciate that he is revered by many as having a higher status than any of the original 12 Apostles. In many people's minds Paul is right in there just below Jesus in a holy "pecking order," yet that does not change the need to justify everything Paul taught after it becomes obvious that some of his teachings directly contradict Jesus. It is possible that Paul assumed he was given the latitude by Jesus' Spirit to organize and teach the churches as he did. It is also possible that Paul did not know everything that Jesus taught. So, I'm looking for reasons for what Paul did in order that he receives the overall credit he deserves. In spite of either of those two hypothetical reasons, even if they did exist, the damage was done by Paul's reported writings nevertheless and it allowed some to take his statements (some, admittedly out of context) and go on to create a religion that Jesus would never recognize. Because some of the messages contained in Paul's writings are so conflicting, it is possible that his original writings could have been tampered with by religious politicians. Frankly, that would make more sense of the mess it's in. However, from whatever the source, the conflicts cannot be tolerated without any inquiry. They should be confronted whether written by Paul or by someone else.

The Paul theologians lead us to believe that <u>The New Testament ushered in a NEW DISPENSATION (Paul's word) which was defined primarily as being the new spiritual components that Paul created and assigned to his version of Christianity</u>. Promotion of Paul's new spirituality by the church institution ultimately had the affect of replacing scripture as being God's guidance for how we live our lives. It was Jesus Himself that said the Holy Spirit would remind us of that guidance; yet that statement by Jesus appears to be unknown within most of today's Christian culture. Instead, The Holy Spirit is largely seen by a new generation as operating in the "now" and in the "future." They are taught to "wing it" beginning with their perception of a "relationship" with Jesus rather than be concerned about any <u>"Old Testament" RULES</u> (Baaaaad words which they denigrate). With that in mind, they ignore the most significant work of the Spirit, which is to illuminate the scriptures to our understanding (John 14:26, Acts 5:32, Ezek. 36:27). Many "new-generation Christians" know very little about what Jesus taught and they have no intention of ever finding out. Their gatherings are similar to high-school pep-rallies and pretty much represents their total "Christian" experience (Not intending disrespect toward them or anyone else who is searching for God….been there….done that). When Paul led us away from the authority of God's inspired word and replaced it with our own understanding, we declared Christianity's God to be different from the God of the Old Testament and the Jews. That has had the affect of establishing a dual God concept. Jesus stated in the 17-18th chapters of John that the only reason He was born was to teach about the righteousness of God. He was referring to the God of the Jews and to the Old Testament when He said that. *(Reference to a dual God concept is not to be confused with the doctrine of the "Trinity" which did not emerge until 400 years after Jesus' death. There, of course, it was concluded by the theologians of that time that God, Jesus and the Holy Spirit were the same and was theorized with the use of Paul's teachings.)*

In spite of what Jesus taught, a large part of Christianity has followed Paul and separated itself from The God of the Jews and we do it in two steps. <u>Step number one</u>: We declare Jesus to be God although He taught they were different (*Ye have heard how I said unto you, I go away, and come again unto you. If ye loved me, ye would rejoice, because I said, **I go unto the Father: for my Father is greater than I.** John 14:28. Also read: John 20:17 and Mark 10:18*). <u>Step number two</u>: We then declare our spiritual connection to Jesus takes precedence over what Jesus taught and was recorded in the four gospels of Matthew, Mark, Luke and John. That, of course, can (as we choose) effectively void any teachings of God the Father as well as Moses, Solomon, Isaiah, Jeremiah and all the other prophets of the Old Testament. Paul's writings enable us to ignore all of that if and when we choose because, after all… Paul has now declared that his new teachings "fulfill" (and obviously becomes a priority over) God's original words recorded in the bible. We, of course, will likely not admit to all of that, but it's nevertheless what we are led to practice in much of today's Christianity. So we each have our own version of God tucked away in a little box somewhere up there in our brain, having strings most definitely attached to our hearts; it's just not always the same God that Jesus taught us about. The God

Jesus was referring to in the book of John was the God of the Old Testament and the Jews and according to Jesus… the God of Christianity is that same God and His commandments of righteousness were written to apply equally to all persons, Jew and Gentile alike. The most significant change that was ever made to the biblical presentation was the path to God through repentance which resulted from a re-designed relationship between man and God and orchestrated by God Himself through the life, ministry, death and resurrection of Jesus as recorded by eyewitness accounts in the four gospels of Matthew, Mark, Luke and John.

Jesus' teachings about that new relationship were initially directed to the Jews. He taught them that salvation was to be by repentance and the continuing pursuit of righteousness. According to Paul's own writing, that is also exactly what Jesus' "Spirit" told Paul to teach to the broader population. Jesus had a single message for everybody: Repent and love God and your neighbor as yourself. The large majority of Jews rejected Jesus and pursued their historical relationship to God. The Jews that rejected Jesus also rejected His salvation. Like most other religions, Judaism has since divided itself into many different factions and Jewish law is now typically viewed as a set of general guidelines rather than a set of restrictions and obligations.

Jews were initially taught by Moses and his successors that the written law itself was legal righteousness and when violated, one could be forgiven with a designated penalty payment similar to a fine for over-parking or speeding. In that situation a person was not being judged on whether or not they actually believed the law they were to practice, just abide by it or pay a penalty. That contrasts with the "New Dispensation," wherein we are now called on to actually believe and endorse God's rules as we practice them (Being born from above).

Jesus changed all the Old Testament standards when He told "The woman at the well" that she didn't know what true worship was and that God was a Spirit who <u>now</u> seeks those to worship Him in Spirit <u>and in truth</u> (The word "Verity" was used to describe "truth" and is translated as "True doctrine"). Although Paul later taught (in some instances) that we do not participate in our salvation, Jesus taught over and over that true righteousness was to be a genuine and sincere goodness, <u>personally</u> experienced and <u>personally</u> expressed toward God and mankind which could only happen through repentance (Learning about and pursuing God's righteousness). <u>That was to be the NEW DISPENSATION and it was defined by Jesus and not by Paul</u>.

Paul initially got it right in his "Sermon on Mars Hill" when he said: *"Forasmuch then as we are the offspring of God, we ought not to think that the Godhead is like unto gold, or silver, or stone, graven by art and man's device. And the times of this ignorance God winked at; but now commandeth all men every where to repent" (Rom.17).*

Although a person's biblical standing with Jehovah/God was obtained through entirely different processes before and after Jesus ministry, God's personality and righteousness never changed; else He would not be God (*"I am the LORD, I change not." Mal 3:5).* After the marvelous statements that Paul made in his "Sermon on Mars Hill," that same Paul went on to later lead us to believe that we are not commanded to pursue the righteousness of God because we are presumed, as a result of God's Grace, to actually and instantly and totally acquire the righteousness of Jesus, just by accepting their teaching that His death was a planned sacrificial offering and substitution (in our place) to God for the forgiveness of all our sins, both past and future. They go on to tell us that that finishes our salvation and the teaching in effect does away with real repentance altogether. When Paul took those positions he had simply ignored that repentance had been established by Jesus as a prerequisite to salvation. Although it was never taught by either Jesus or by God that Jesus' death was to be a substitute for repentance that is the bottom line of what Paul taught. Paul, along with current well known evangelists such as Billy Graham, cover their bases by teaching repentance with passion, while in practice not requiring any application of it. Billy Graham taught Paul's version of the gospel almost exclusively. Graham preaches Jesus' "NAME" loudly while concurrently teaching a completely differing gospel.... according to "Paul."

Remembering again that according to Paul himself, when Jesus' Spirit gave Paul the specific assignment of "Minister" to the Gentiles, this is what Paul was charged with:

> *"To open their eyes, and to **TURN** them from darkness to light, and from the power of Satan unto God, that they*

may receive forgiveness of sins, and inheritance among them which are sanctified by faith that is in Me (Acts 26:18)."

It is interesting to note (and remember) in this quotation what Jesus said about how a person "may receive forgiveness of sins." This was reported by Paul to have been spoken to him by Jesus' Spirit 37 years <u>after He was crucified and was resurrected</u> and Paul reported that in this encounter Jesus continued to tie salvation directly to repentance and the pursuit of righteous living and those conditions apply to this date. He had spoken of it in times past as being "born again" (or born from above). Jesus never-ever said that by "receiving Him and His sacrificial death as being a payment (to God) for our present and future sins" or "inviting Him to come into our heart" would initiate salvation. It was Paul that led some of us to believe that…. and that's also what I was taught. I was led to direct my "faith" toward a spiritual "image" of Jesus that had been created primarily to engage and direct my emotions while ignoring most of the things Jesus had actually taught. Jesus instructed Paul to teach the Gentiles about the deity of God and about Himself and to teach them God's standards for living their life…period. Jesus' instructions were simple: Love God and Love each other. The only standard to achieve perfect harmony was "Do unto others as you would have them do unto you." Within that standard lies God's formula for success. Outside of it lies conflict and struggle in the biblical man-God relationship because "God is love."

Over the centuries, many bible manipulators have used Paul as their primary source to pattern after. However, they changed some of what Paul taught as well as changed or ignored other teachings from God and Jesus. Using their "brand-new" bibles, they created a new and far more complicated religion that carried forth the name of Jesus Christ while ignoring most everything He taught and eventually died for. I admit the new bibles are really cool and it's intriguing to compare the 1611 KJV to revised manuscripts which were created by skilled politicians just over the last 400 years. Over time, changing just a single word here and there re-writes it all. As an example: The issue of whether or not God is routinely and continually interactive down to the personal level was changed by the mere changing of one word. In the widely used reference to Jeremiah 29:11 they changed the word "thoughts" to "plan" which set the practice of Christianity on a new path and that's only one example of many changes. They changed the Bible to make it read the way they wanted it to read.

It is also interesting to witness the redesigned "Christian" community that has emerged from it all. Their philosophy was simple. It was to embrace cultural shifts so progressive societies would be comfortable with whatever god-image was presented to them. A changing of culture could reduce church attendance and that could reduce cash flow; so, they addressed that problem by changing the God image to suit whatever the current evolving culture required God to be (They ignored what God had said about that: *"I am the LORD, I change not." Mal 3:5)* Beginning with Paul, it has always been about "giving them what they want" and we will discover that is exactly how Paul achieved much of his success. Want another God? You got it!

The current attitudes coming from many young liberal Paul oriented "Christians" include: "Tradition is stupid" and "Old is bad" and some of them apply it not only to history in general, but more specifically to the Constitution of the United States as well as to the Bible. Some attempt to construct what they refer to as "social justice" within the liberal political arena while disregarding any input from scripture. Jesus declared God and politics to be different domains and taught that social justice is to be pursued first-of-all on a personal one-on-one level. He did not envision that His gospel would be declared through government organizations, rather by individuals in the way they live their lives (When ye do it unto them, ye also do it unto me). Many believe they are practicing Christianity by supporting socialist governments and their benevolent agendas while never lifting one finger to personally do anything for anybody.

It appears that their "new-generation Christianity" eliminates the stigma of scripture altogether. They have simplified it to the falling in love between two spirits. Although they proudly declare their new generation, they obviously have no concern that Christianity has been redesigned just for them and the culture they hold to. There are some who's greatest misconception is that intellect has advanced along with technology when in fact; having use of it has had the opposite effect. It's easy to become a clone to the culture it has created. They at times appear to believe that their having use of the latest technology somehow elevates them above those who invented it. Their perception of life can easily be defined just by observing some of their favorite television programs. Although the programming I am referring to is for the most part pure fantasy, it is nevertheless called "REALITY." That could qualify them as being "The fantasy generation." They don't seem to know or understand that human nature has changed very little over the history of mankind and that playing with a new hi-tech toy doesn't necessarily elevate them to a higher plateau of understanding than that of some ancient cave-man. I would never negatively diminish their zeal nor their energy nor their personal motives because I was also once part of a new generation that considered its self unique and different and I understand what it's about. However, on a worldwide scale, Christianity's current fall from grace can be traced directly to the ungodly culture its own members have helped create. Their culture is all about feeling good about "ME." They just like having their back scratched and can be led to just about anywhere by a good back scratcher.

At times it's not altogether a person's fault they practice that principle because (with exceptions of course) "I want it and I want it now" has been taught and demonstrated to children for the last two generations. As the practice evolves, child-worship may naturally become an extension of self-worship and is perceived to be normal by those who play the game. (No, I do not hate children) To love a child is normal. To worship a child may be more about you than about them. ("Look what I made"). Those who practice it will, of course, deny both.

What's any of that got to do with Paul, you ask? It was Paul that subtlety led us away from scripture and its culture into the fantasy-land of a "create your own God" mentality. The God some of us went on to create turned out to be a God named "Me" and "Mine" and that becomes the only God we worship. Many church programs appear to be developed around that presumption with sermons sounding more like bedtime stories, embellished with all kind of goodies and treats and play periods and entertainment at every gathering. Most everyone feels at home in that environment because we quite naturally pursue the fun we are accustomed to... anywhere we find it.

Although the belief about and practice of traditional Christianity is declining worldwide, many of those followers of Paul appear to have no personal concerns about it and it speaks to their fundamental insincerity about the personalized God image they hold to. For starters, it's almost as if they have no knowledge of the history of Christianity. Although it doesn't appear to matter to them about what's going on outside their own world of "self," some pastors of local churches appear to be content with it all as long as their local "church operation" remains profitable. With personal spirituality now being the central format, their primary emphasis is directed more to the church's social activities and entertainment rather than teaching about and pursuing God's righteousness. Along with that, we have also been unwittingly programmed by religious political correctness to tolerate anything, including our own destruction. They truly did a number on us. We have been beat down and are afraid of expressing any independent thought or analysis concerning anything directed at us. We become terrified that we may be perceived as being "judgmental." We seem to survive and sometimes even thrive when we're together doing all those fun little things we do; but fail the Christian test as individuals when we are out in the rest of society....out there where our little light is supposed to shine. To me, "Shinning our little light" is not about going around waving a Jesus flag and announcing: "Thank you Jesus" for the many blessings (miracles) you keep sending my way (God knows I deserve each and every one). Shinning that light has more to do with how we show respect for other people and specifically what we do in our relationships with them. Unfortunately, many that do shine their light, shines it on Paul's teachings and not on Jesus' teachings. Because of that as well as our nonchalant and timid existence, we are losing our Christian culture and we are losing our country and it all started at Paul's institution of the church.

If we assume the spirit of God (The Holy Spirit) did not lead Paul to teach anything contradictory to Jesus' teachings, then in those particular instances Paul himself just made them up. They were not from The Holy Spirit, not from Jesus and not from God. That being agreed to, would it not bring into question other teachings from Paul? How could we ever accept any new doctrine that Paul teaches as being an expansion of God's revelation to mankind while he, at the same time, contradicts many things that God and Jesus taught? The Paul factor, if studied faithfully, could bring down some of Christianity's "Institutionalized" man-made doctrines toward the simple messages Jesus taught: "Love

God and Love your neighbor as yourself." There are many who believe they are followers of Jesus, when in fact they actually follow a combination of doctrines that originated with The "Apostle" Paul with alterations over the years by John Calvin, Rick Warren and others. It can be said that Paul invented the Institution that went on to assume control over the Church and that Paul is the architect of Christianity as we know it. In order to verify that conclusion we will reference some high profile teachings by Paul which obviously contradict the Biblical God and Jesus.

In my book "A View from the Pew" (page 33) I described some of the results Paul's teachings have had on many church doctrines:

"The foundation and life blood of the business-approach, growth-oriented, INSTITUTION-CONTROLLED church organizations are contained in and completely dependent on, their unrelenting promotion of the following doctrines:

1. God has, in advance, determined a complete plan for each individual's life; and through His miraculous hands-on intervention, micro-manages every detail of each person's life experience…..WRONG! According to original scripture.

2. Redefines the role and purpose of prayer, and then uses prayer as one method of influencing and/or controlling the church membership……WRONG! According to original scripture

3. Emphasizes our connection to The Holy Spirit, while at the same time minimizes an equal value to knowing and understanding all scripture......WRONG! According to original scripture.

4. The Tithe is mandated for New Testament Christians and is to be collected by anyone claiming to have God's approval....WRONG! According to original scripture.

5. Church leadership has been given Biblical authority over its membership......WRONG! According to original scripture."

We easily recognize those definitions of the Church and Christianity because many of us have grown-up under their directives. They are attributable to a combination of origins with the Apostle Paul at the top of the list.

We should give Paul all the bows and accolades he deserves. Let's also be honest about the origin of everything he wrote and taught. There is no question that Paul faithfully wrote and taught many truthful words of instruction concerning God the Father and Jesus Christ. He presented an awesome characterization of God in his "Sermon on Mars Hill" (Acts 17:22-31) and in other places made marvelous statements of truth that lined-up with the rest of what God and Jesus had taught. But we cannot be distracted by that. The fact that Paul taught truth in some instances does not give him license to teach half-truths and lies in others. That is the textbook way deceit is presented and once confirmed, casts doubt on all the rest.

Paul taught as Jesus taught on many important subjects but then went on to contradict those same teachings in other positions he would take. He taught the significance and power of "The Word" while elsewhere relegating it to secondary importance. He taught righteous living as being a standard while in other places claiming it to be impossible. If one studies Paul carefully, we see that his "yes-you-can, no-you-can't" approach to defining Christian principles is a distraction from the specific messages Jesus would have us learn. Jesus' messages were simple and they were not multiple-choice.

Paul had a unique way of not dealing directly with issues with his "both sides of his mouth" style of teaching. As one of many examples he said in 1st Cor. 1:27: *"But God hath chosen the foolish things of the world to confound the wise,"* but then went on to also say: *"God is not the author of confusion"* (1st Cor. 14:33). Such "free-wheeling" declarations by Paul are taught with passion from behind pulpits and no one ever seems to connect the dots. That pattern occurs throughout Paul's teachings.

Paul was into organizing an institution and it appears that the dynamics of Paul's Church-building zeal resulted in the creation of Institutionalism which still rides herd over the church organizations of today. Policies established by various denominational institutions are directly reflected in how their congregations live their lives and treat others and at times it's difficult to find Jesus among them.

Under Paul's leadership, it appears the early churches were just unwilling to practice or pursue righteousness and were unwilling to purge unrighteousness from their ranks of church leadership as taught in scripture (Luke 12:57, Mat. 18:15-17, 1st Pet. 4:17). Apparently Paul could not contain that "leaven" (unrighteousness) in the expanding church community and it appears he made up his own rules to settle disputes while continuing to give priority to growing the movement. In order to deal with his congregation's colliding attitudes, Paul (generally from long distances) began to compromise what Jesus taught about pursuing righteousness and instead went on to teach if a person is "in Christ," God then sees them as being righteous just as they are. It is not clear that Paul ever explained all of what it means to be "in Christ" outside of his personal definition and promotion of a spiritual connection. That is where the emphasis remains to this day, yet many somehow come to believe they are "In Christ" while still treating each other like dirt.

The following teaching by Paul is one of many statements he made which illustrates why many give "learning from God's Spirit" priority over "Learning from God's word:"

> *"Now we have received, not the spirit of the world, but the spirit which is of God; that we might know the things that are freely given to us of God." "Which things also we speak, not in the words which man's wisdom teacheth, but which the Holy Ghost teacheth; comparing spiritual things with spiritual.* (1st Cor. 2:12-13)

For some, that teaching (and others) had the affect of discounting much of God's Word already recorded in scripture. For starters, Paul declared through his writings that he was personally taught doctrines by Jesus' Spirit which actually contradicted what had already been spoken by Jesus and documented by the eye witness experiences of Matthew, Mark, Luke and John. Although Jesus said The Holy Spirit would remind us of His teachings, for many followers of Paul, their perceived Spiritual connection to Jesus never serves to remind them of anything Jesus had previously taught. Furthermore, they do not appear to believe that recorded scripture is to be given priority in the way they live their lives because they now get that either directly from their perception of Jesus' Spirit or from a storyteller behind a pulpit.

It appears by his multiple-choice approach to teaching righteous living Paul was telling them what they wanted to hear. On the other hand, he went on to establish ridged rules of his own that gave authority to church leaders and created a governing system to enforce them. Paul was a politician.

The Roman Catholic Church eventually emerged out of the early Christian organizational chaos, with its foundation being the office of "Bishop of Rome." The office was held by the Apostle Peter, who is claimed to be the first Pope by that church. Many successive Popes, each one assuming absolute and total power at their personal and independent discretion, went on to dramatically change Peter's doctrines to suit themselves. The Roman Catholic movement became widespread as a result of the power and expansive reach of The

Roman Empire, coupled with the promotion of Christianity by Emperor Constantine the 1st. It was the politician Constantine along with Iranaeus, Bishop of Lyons, who at the council of Nicaea used their influence to hand-pick the four gospels which were allowed to become part of the official Bible. The Gospels they rejected are an interesting read, some having been set aside for almost 2000 years without being tampered with by religious politicians. After "Nicaea," all other gospels were declared to be heresy and were almost completely destroyed except for those few which were hidden in caves for centuries. I think the gospel of Thomas is the most significant. It would benefit a follower of Jesus to research and read the lost gospels in spite of the church institutions' opposition to them.

Out of that initial <u>government oriented</u>/<u>government-controlled</u> "Christian" movement emerged independent spin-offs with reform after reform, being, of course, the Protestants. The Catholics followed principally after Peter while acknowledging Paul and the Protestants followed principally after Paul while acknowledging Peter. Neither the Catholics nor the Protestants followed after Jesus when it came to their exercise of power and control over the congregations, as well as other matters. They both ignored many things Jesus taught and went on to create "Ole Wives Tale" doctrines that became significant trademarks of their respective institutions. Each of their leaderships eventually re-wrote the Bible to suit their selves, disagreeing on things as fundamental as "The Ten Commandments." Many Churches in the 21st Century now appear more as businesses than churches of Jesus Christ;

however, there are a few jewels here and there that shine among them and still proclaim the Word of God as it is written and intended to be read.

Unfortunately, the Apostle Paul's influence on the Christian movement started-off on the wrong foot and because of it much of the so-called Christian community is still marching out of step almost 2000 years later. Paul's multiple-choice approach to Jesus' "Do unto others" mandate led many away from what Jesus taught to a virtual "Create your own God" mentality.

When Paul stated that "All scripture is given by the inspiration of God" he should not have contradicted so much of it in his own writings. I would guess that the majority of Paul's early converts not only did not themselves have a copy of the Old Testament books, but were also unaware of the details of "The Four Gospels," yet to be written by Matthew, Mark, Luke and John. So, what Paul taught them would have been for the most part all they got and they more than likely did not know the specifics of Jesus teachings except as they heard it from Paul. Consequently, they had little or nothing to compare Paul's teachings with. Although many of us are aware that Paul taught differently than Jesus on specific issues, we still have a tendency to give Paul the "nod" when push comes to shove and that's because <u>we have been taught to be followers of Paul…not Jesus</u>. Many of our teachers insinuate that Paul's teachings were indorsed by Jesus, but that is not true for those specific ones we will highlight.

Generally speaking, the Jesus franchise draws a crowd who are then taught to become followers of Paul. Many of us will sing praises to Jesus and will pray to Jesus and will wear T-shirts with Jesus' name on the front and the back and will wear WWJD bracelets (What would Jesus do?) and will wear the cross symbol around our necks; but when it comes to living our lives as well as identifying ourselves with God, we follow Paul's teachings, period.

Paul's writings were either inspired by The Holy Spirit or else he made them up, or both. If both, how do we know when he was and when he wasn't being taught by God's Spirit? The answer to that is: "Only when his writings are verified by what God and Jesus taught in the rest of scripture." After all, Paul was to carry forth their messages, not contradict them. According to Paul, he was appointed by Jesus as a "minister" to do that alone. It is possible that a person such as Paul can be inspired by God's Spirit to know and dispense God's truth and at the same time make errors that may be mistaken as being inspired by God. Both Kings David and Solomon were good examples of that. Even Moses made errors by failing to follow God's instructions. So, we have to do what Paul taught Timothy: "Rightly divide the word of truth;" and we can start off by questioning many things Paul himself taught. Remember first and foremost what Jesus taught and that should be our standard:***"If ye continue in My word, then are ye My disciples indeed; and ye shall know the truth, and the truth shall make you free.….If the Son therefore shall make you free, ye shall be free indeed."*** *John 8:31-32 & 36*. That is the only rule to follow in dealing with the Paul dilemma.

So, what do we do with that large amount of the New Testament that Paul wrote, some will ask? Without question, we have to give weight to Paul's teachings. Some of them are truthfully and wonderfully expressed. It is my thought when we find that Paul's teachings contradict those of God the Father and Jesus we give priority to what God and Jesus taught and in those instances completely discount what Paul taught. Clergy should be helping us do that. Also, any other teaching by Paul which is not confirmed by God and/or Jesus becomes suspect. How else can it be treated?

When Paul wrote that "all scripture is inspired by God," the New Testament writings had not yet been consolidated and it naturally falls that Paul was referring to the Old Testament. There was a lot of tampering with scripture in the early days (as is the case today) and as a result it's possible that Paul could have been misquoted, either as the New Testament was being formed or without doubt....later revised. So, in this situation we should give weight to Paul's advice which is confirmed by what God and Jesus taught. A general approach to Paul's teachings should be, as with other scripture, when it is not clearly stated and/or verified, we are to pray that God's Spirit will illuminate its validity and meaning.

As a result of Paul's ministry, Jesus' personal mission to teach the pursuit of "righteousness" was ultimately redefined through Paul's teachings from "Do unto others" to "Go to Church." The same folks that led us to establish that personal relationship with Jesus go on from there to promote the support of the Institution of the church and its programs as being both the foundation and the definition of the Christian life. If today a person is thought of as being a "practicing" Christian, they are perceived to be a person who supports some church organization…period. Just how or what that person "does unto others" never comes into play. Some churches cover their bases by informally endorsing the "golden rule" while silently observing their congregations' flagrant ignoring of it. I know many people who believe they are totally fulfilling Jesus' teachings only by their attendance and support of a church in which they are a member. To some, God is just a "bee-bop" away and as far as they are concerned He begins and ends with the music. It's much easier to "Go to Church" than to "Do unto others." There's nothing wrong, of course, in doing both; but if "going to church" doesn't produce the "do unto others" mandate given by Jesus, it's a waste of time to go there except for the social aspects of it. Paul is the only Bible character that taught we should routinely go to church (Do not forsake the assembling of yourselves together). Jesus taught the "woman at the well" that she didn't have to go anywhere to worship God. He also told her she had no idea how to worship or who she was worshipping. (John 4:19-26)

On a more positive note, history tells us that one will likely find kindred spirits in a church organization whose friendships last a lifetime and that's the primary reason some folks I know still go to their church. It's the social life stupid! The sad thing is, I believe some churches are satisfied with that as being the primary reason for our attendance. Although those friendships draw us there, along the way we must not get confused when it comes to the so-called Christian doctrine being presented to us while we're doing fun time with our friends. Many churches use those "play periods" to lead us directly to Paul, not to Jesus and we must not forget that "Jesus" merely stamped on our foreheads may not, by itself, influence either our hearts or our minds or our life or our future. Being a supporting "church member" does not, by its self, fulfill our personal responsibility to "do unto others as we would have them do unto us;" never did, never will. Some believe their church's outreach programs fulfill all personal Christian obligations. There is something magnetic that draws us to group worship which at times takes precedence over the doctrines being taught there. It's a phenomenon called "groupthink." Although "groupthink" may control the narrative, a Collective practice of Christianity doesn't fully count unless its primary purpose has been directed to the personal application of a Christian life to those outside the church house as well to those inside. If "my little light" isn't shining outside as well as to those inside (personally between me and every other person I come in contact with) I could be disconnected from the power source altogether.

Paul's dedication to his own mission is not in question. His overall achievement of it as well as his lack of achievement and how they both influenced the development of Christianity and the Church is what we are exploring. He may have believed everything he taught was from God but that doesn't make it so. Having key doctrines designed by Paul and installed within the institution, the so-called "church" went on to assume life and death powers normally assigned to governments. In some instances the early "church" co-existed with government to share total rule over the State. People who disagreed with the "church" were sometimes imprisoned and/or executed. The "church" even created armies that fought wars around the world in the name of Jesus.

Paul's so-called "church" also went on to accumulate great wealth and power and some of its leaders lived like kings (as some still do today). Paul's teachings took priority over Jesus' teachings beginning all the way back to 60-70 AD when he invented the Institution that took control over his church. Paul's church institution has formulated a spirit-based spirit-driven movement that was perpetuated over the centuries by newly formed and ever enlarging generations who were led to be followers of Paul from one generation to the next. Paul obviously could not have anticipated that such havoc would accompany the changing of just one rule which was firmly installed by Jesus, a rule that declared church leadership was not to "rule" over the congregations. But that was just the beginning of "The Paul factor;" Christianity is still struggling to accept the simple messages that Jesus would have us learn, messages such as: *"My yoke is easy, and My burden is light;"* just *"love God and Do unto others as you would have them do unto you."*

Some of Paul's doctrines have already been highlighted in the introductory remarks. The following is documentation in connection with those as well as some of his other teachings, all of which directly contradicted Jesus:

ABOUT THE AUTHORITY OF CHURCH LEADERSHIP

Jesus never envisioned a bureaucratic form of government taking authority over His followers. He specifically instructed the following in Mathew 20:25-27:

> *"You know that the princes of the Gentiles <u>exercise dominion</u> over them, and they that are great <u>exercise authority</u> upon them. But **<u>it shall not be so among you</u>**. But whosoever will be great **<u>among you</u>**, let him be your minister; and whosoever will be chief **<u>among you</u>**, let him be your servant."*

Paul taught the opposite to those clear instructions that had been given by Jesus.

When Paul invented the "Institution" (organizational structure) and put it in charge of church groups, he established control over the congregations through designated leaders assigned to leadership positions in each group. Based on church history, those individual leaders obviously went on to expand their own personal interpretation of the initial authority Paul had given them. Paul established a bureaucratic authority designed to accompany the organized Church congregations and that authority remains in a subtle but controlling form to this day. Although church leadership tries to dispel the notion, there is a glass ceiling between the pulpit and the pews. Little or no discussions exist in church groups about scripture or doctrine and many of them still function under some of the original rules that Paul established. This is some of what Paul taught the church congregations:

> *"Remember them which have the rule over you, who have spoken unto you the word of God... Obey them that have that rule over you, and submit yourselves: for they watch for your souls." (Hebrews 13:7 & 17)*

In an effort to completely change the meaning of that scripture, revisionists eliminated the words "who have spoken to you the word of God" and replaced it with such things as: "it was they who brought you." They also replaced: "for they watch for your souls" with: "They are like men standing guard over your spiritual good." It was pretty sneaky to change the original text from its obvious initial reference to "clergy" in order to teach that Paul was referring to "civil authorities." All of those revisions have been made by modern Christian revisionists in order to deny the "iron fist" control Paul initially established over the congregations.

Paul also wrote:

> *"Let every soul be subject unto the higher powers. For there is no power but of God: the powers that be are ordained of God. Whosoever therefore resisteth the power, resisteth*

the <u>ordinance of God</u>: and they that resist shall receive to themselves damnation. For rulers are not a terror to good works, but to the evil. Wilt thou then not be afraid of the power? do that which is good, and thou shalt have praise of the same: For <u>he is the minister of God</u> to thee for good. But if thou do that which is evil, be afraid; for he beareth not the sword in vain: for <u>he is the minister of God</u>, a revenger to execute wrath upon him that doeth evil. Wherefore ye must needs be subject, not only for wrath, but also for conscience sake." (Romans 13:1-5)

In spite of Paul's original statement which was clearly referring to Church leaders, over the years I was taught that this "Romans" quotation also applies only to political authorities outside the church. The 12th chapter of Romans is all about the function of the church and the 13th chapter continues that dialog. Paul referred to church leaders there (12th Chapter) as "Ministers of God," which was consistent with what he also taught in the 13th Chapter of Hebrews. Paul's references to "rule" and "rulers" in both the book of Romans as well as the book of Hebrews gave authority to successive Church rulers that not only accepted Paul's mandate, but went on to later expand that authority to assume and practice life and death powers over the congregations.

The indisputable history of what actually happened in the early churches should by itself confirm to us that Paul did indeed establish power over the congregations and that he was indeed referring to Church leaders in both above scripture references. Paul gave them the initial controlling authority and history confirms that they took that control and ultimately expanded it for a period of time to a total dictatorial level. How else could the church institution have turned so quickly to such mayhem in the very early days of Christianity except through Paul's initial authority?

Later revisionists, wanting to exonerate Paul, attempted to change those passages of scripture so they would not be interpreted as applying to church leaders. They changed key words which completely changed their original apparent meaning. It was a cover-up in an attempt to put the early history of the church in order. In the Romans 13:1-5 scripture reference, several revised bibles eliminated the word "minister" and used either "agent" or "servant" in its place. Other specific revisions eliminated the word "minister" and in its place changed it to read: "The authorities that are over him," "The authorities of government," "It's lawful Superiors." "The governing authorities," "The government that is over him," "For the magistrate is God's minister to thee for good," "For they are God's servants appointed for your good," and on and on. One revisionist was so blatant as to change the word "minister" to read: "the **civil** authorities are God's official servants faithfully devoting themselves to this very end." (The New Testament: A translation in the language of the People. Richard Francis Weymouth.)

To illustrate the lingering affect of erroneous teaching resulting from bible revision, I personally heard two well known pastors in the Dallas-Ft Worth area preach similar sermons on 11/11/12 (first Sunday after the presidential election) admonishing each of their audiences that based upon scripture, Obama was selected by God to his second term as President and we are to honor God's choice. That is absurd. In addition to their references to Old Testament statements back when God actually chose who would be King among the Jews, they went on to use Hebrews 13 and Romans 13 as their authority to extend God's practice of selecting ruling Kings to a current status. It is my opinion that both pastors relied on their audiences' inability or unwillingness to research what the Bible actually teaches about it. It should have been an insult to anyone in their audiences who had knowledge of original scripture.

Remembering that *"God is not the author of confusion,"* that advice from the two reverends becomes laughable because it does not jive with anything we've ever learned about politicians. Most are generally interested in promoting their own welfare rather than ours and that applies particularly to Obama. Politicians are ministers of God? Based on what we all know about politicians that would be very confusing to be coming from a God who is not the author of confusion. It came entirely from bible revisions.

If one assumes that Paul had actually intended that the above two quoted bible references were referring to governmental rulers instead of Church rulers that would have also been contrary to Jesus' teaching for another reason. Jesus had already declared them to be different domains when He said: "Render unto Caesar what is Caesar's and to God what is God's." Paul then would have been declaring them to be in partnership (Politics and Religion), just the opposite of what Jesus taught. Paul would have been wrong no matter which of the two positions he could have taken about who should rule because Jesus had already declared that no one should rule. There is no question that organization and leadership was necessary; however, church leaders were to become servants, not rulers and that's where Paul "missed the boat." Jesus' intentions were that Church leadership was to be by consent and not by rule.

And finally, the Apostle Peter, who was selected by Jesus to build His church, taught the following in 1st Peter 1:13-15:

> *"Submit yourselves to every ordinance of man for the Lord's sake: whether it be to the king, as supreme; Or unto governors, as unto them that are sent by him for the punishment of evildoers, and for the praise of them that do well. For so is the will of God, that with well doing ye may put to silence the ignorance of foolish men"*

In this writing, Peter did not teach that God hand-picks the kings of this world, nor do I believe that Paul was suggesting it either. Paul was referring to church leaders only.

As church organizations grew, Paul's leaders and those that followed them went on to set more ridged rules and mete-out punishments for those who violated them. They became absolute rulers over the church. Those that disagreed with them were treated harshly. They put people in prison and also put people to death. They gathered armies and fought wars.

The early history of Christianity teaches us that Paul clearly established a bureaucracy that over time became an oppressive in-house government which was designed to control the church and was totally contrary to what Jesus taught.

About The Role
Of Women In
Church Gatherings

The Apostle Paul taught that there were different standards between men and women when it came to church gatherings. Their teaching and discussions about scripture and observance of ordinances were to be carried out by the men only. The women were told to sit down and shut up. They were told if they had any questions about what was going on they were to wait until they got home and then they could ask their husbands to explain it to them. The Apostle Paul, architect of Christian "Church Institutionalism," started off with similar rules about women that the Muslim faith endorses to this day.

Paul taught the following:

> *"Let your women keep silence in the churches: for it is not permitted unto them to speak; but they are commanded to be under obedience as also saith the law. And if they will learn any thing, let them ask their husbands at home: for it is a shame for women to speak in the church."* 1 Cor. 14:35-36

> *"Let the woman learn in silence with all subjection. But I suffer not a woman to teach, nor to usurp authority over the man, but to be in silence."* 1st Tim. 2:11-12

Paul obviously adopted the governing law or custom in that region and applied it to the church when he said *"as also sayeth the law."* The slavish rules that Paul arbitrarily brought into the church congregations were the very opposite to the freedom and equality that Jesus had brought to women. When he began bringing local culture into the church and adopting it as having a legitimate standing in Christian philosophy and doctrine, he turned the church away from the biblical Jesus toward his own presumptions.

It was inappropriate for Paul to advocate bringing existing cultures into the requirements and functions of the church and I believe this further illustrates we are not to believe and practice what a person who claims to be called by God teaches when it contradicts what God or Jesus taught or implied. That not only applies to Paul but also to the religious icons of our time. If we are to believe ourselves to be Christians, the biblical supported standards established by God the Father and by Jesus must have priority over all others and we must measure everything we are being taught in sermons and songs by comparing and using those standards. "Why, I never heard of such a thing," "You're no fun at all," I can hear some say.

Scripture teaches us that some of God's other chosen people also made mistakes. In this instance, Paul had no right to declare women second class Christians. He was called by Jesus to take the gospel to the gentiles and Jesus did not intend that Paul sit the women on the back row with duck tape across their mouths. (I'll bet you didn't know that "duck-tape" was invented by Paul almost two thousand years ago just for that purpose).

The following (expanded) statement by Paul in 1st Tim. 2:11-15 illustrates the origin of his beliefs about women:

> *"Let the woman learn in silence with all subjection. But I suffer not a woman to teach, nor to usurp authority over the man, but to be in silence. For Adam was first formed, then Eve. And Adam was not deceived, but the woman being deceived was in the transgression. Notwithstanding she shall be saved in childbearing, if they continue in faith and charity and holiness with sobriety."*

She made me do it? Did Paul relegate women to 2nd class or what?

The fact that most churches later ignored this teaching by Paul confirms these conclusions about it.

I have heard some Christians, who want to give Paul a pass on this one, say that Paul was addressing the chattering habit of some women and was just telling them to tone it down a bit when church is going on. Read the above bible quotations again. It doesn't say that. It tells all women they are to be passive bystanders when in church and if they want to learn anything about what goes on there to wait until they get home and ask their husbands to teach them about it. The misgiving of those Christians who would give Paul a pass about what he obviously said is an example of how some "pooh-pooh" or ignore any scripture that contradicts the institution's current "enlightenment" or "practice." Some of Paul's other doctrines are so well received that they are just willing to ignore this one.

When Jesus addressed the crowds that followed Him, He never differentiated between the men and the women, both of which were in His audience. All of His teachings were addressed to everyone equally. He never even hinted that men and women had different value, in or out of a church house. Since Jesus teachings were contrary to what Paul taught, is it possible that at a particular point in time and because of political pressure from some men within the congregations, these strange rules were established by Paul in order to silence the "squeaky wheel" demands that women observe the culture of the day both in and out of church? What other reason could there have been? That would imply nothing has changed in 2000 years. Today's "Church" organizations continue to scramble to make room for evolving cultures (Give them what they want. Tell them what they want to hear). Here again, this highlights the inconsistency in Paul's teachings because he made no distinction between male and female standings on numerous other occasions in New Testament writings such as in Eph. 4:4-6 and Col. 3:16. Maybe this was directed only to the people in Corinth and to Timothy, without considering that all his letters would eventually be grouped together in a Bible format and compared side by side. A different doctrine for different crowds is also not a very good way to promote Christianity and it could have all started with Paul.

ABOUT CLASS DISTINCTION WITHIN GOD'S FAMILY

It is stated in Acts 10: *Then Peter opened his mouth, and said, Of a truth I perceive that God is no respecter of persons: But in every nation he that feareth him, and worketh righteousness, is accepted with him. The word which God sent unto the children of Israel, preaching peace by Jesus Christ: (he is Lord of all:)*

Jesus Himself said: *"Come unto Me, **all ye** that labour and are heavy laden, and I will give you rest. Take my yoke upon you, and learn of Me, for I am meek and lowly in heart: and ye shall find rest unto your souls. For My yoke is easy, and My burden is light."* (Mat. 11:28-30)

Paul, on the other hand, would make <u>married</u> women subject to their husband's total authority. There is a subtlety attached to Paul's independent and totally different teachings which suggests that Jesus' teachings were directed to Jews only. As an example, Paul instructed in the 5th chapter of Ephesians: *"A husband is in charge of his wife in the same way Christ is in charge of His body the Church. So, you wives must willingly obey your husband in everything, just as the Church obeys Christ."* Jesus never taught such a thing. Paul has insinuated here that married women were not even considered part of the church. He (Paul) had already declared married women as being a second class member of God's family in matters concerning the church and now carries it further by requiring women to obey their husbands within their personal relationships apart from church. It would have been better to have taught "Do unto others as you would have them do unto you." as the basis for a happy marriage as well as equal participation in the life of the church. That would work much better. Jesus was right. Paul was wrong.

ABOUT SELF-WORTH

Self-love is the natural result of being a living creature. Jesus would have us extend the intensity of that love to others while Paul would convert it to serfdom. This is just another of their differing views which could not be more conflicting.

Considering the range of human emotions, those elements of "free spirit," "self-love," "self-respect," and "mercy," properly blended together, determine how we see other people and the world around us. It also very specifically determines how we visualize the God-man relationship. It is not surprising then that religious politicians would attempt to define each of them for us, nudging us in the direction they would have us go. Paul "wrote the book" on just how that is done as he developed his own version of the gospel.

Jesus taught a very positive message about the value of the individual and one's self–worth. According to scripture, when Jesus was sent by God the Father to rescue fallen mankind, He announced: *"I am come that they might have life, and that they might have it more abundantly."* (John 10:10) Jesus went on to teach: *"If you continue in My word, then you are My disciples indeed; and you shall know the truth, and the truth shall make you free…..If the Son therefore shall make you free, you shall be free indeed."* (John 8:31-32 & 36)

Jesus teaching "Do unto others as you would have them do unto you" was emphasized by Him as being both the cornerstone and the keystone to all scripture and spoke directly to the value of each person, male and female alike. Jesus always called the shots as He saw them and it was seldom done in a "lowliness of mind" fashion. He taught us that other people are to be treated with respect and as our equal and that it should not diminish our own self-image as we do it. That's what Jesus did when it was deserved and He did it from strength, not weakness.

Paul, on the other hand, having already declared women as being second class when it came to matters of the Church and of their marriages, went on to broadly teach:

> *"Let nothing be done through strife or vainglory; but in lowliness of mind let each esteem other better than themselves."* (Phil. 2:3-4)

Paul went on to state in verse 5 that this represented the mind of Jesus even though Jesus never taught such a thing in the four gospels, nor is it taught anywhere else in scripture. That teaching is without doubt a "Paul-ism." It appears innocent enough on the surface but it was apparently designed by Paul to discourage an inquisitive or independent attitude among the brethren. Paul had already declared that everyone was to submit to their own Church leaders and was now attempting to cultivate an even more submissive attitude among and between the congregations. He was clearly attempting to create congregations of servants to the church institution and if one looks closely at what he was teaching, it flies directly in the face of the Jesus "Do unto others" doctrine. Everyone wins with "Do unto others" and we do it without any "lowliness of mind" toward each other.

It would be difficult for a true child of God to think of their selves in such low esteem as Paul would have it. The bible teaches we are to first be humble before God. Then it teaches we are to treat each other with respect. As Paul established church congregations, he elevated his "submissive-humility" concept to a high pedestal in his personal definition of virtue and righteousness. The absolute application of such a rule is opposed to man's natural self-preservation instinct. Man's natural instinct is to experience total humility only toward something or someone that has irresistible and unquestionable power over us. In that situation it can be said that humility almost borders on fear. So, what Paul was teaching ran counter to man's nature because his teaching: *"in lowliness of mind let each esteem other better than themselves"* suggests it is possible to also experience humility toward weakness as well as irresistible power. How does that work? We can be very kind to a person who we see and know to be weak and do good deeds toward them without feeling any humility at all; and we do those good deeds without regard to any comparative feelings we have judged toward them. We do it without experiencing "lowliness of mind" and we do it without "esteeming" them to be higher or lower than ourselves. We can do those kind things because we believe we are God's emissaries. That's the source of our self-worth. We are God's children and God's children are heirs to the kingdom of God.

In the meantime, just how did the subject of "Self worth" evolve to the subject of "Humility" you ask? I'm glad you asked that question. Some would declare the promotion of "self worth" as being totally contrary to the whole notion of being "humble." They seem to be suggesting that we can't be a humble person if we begin thinking of our self as being too important or too worthy before God. They insinuate that God loves us only because we are trash. According to scripture we have two choices: attempt to become the humble acting person that Paul has declared we should become or remember what Jesus said: *"If the Son therefore shall make you free, you shall be free indeed."* It's harder to act humble when you're free.

Humility is not something a person has to cultivate; it comes with the territory if one truly believes there is a God. That, in itself, is the ultimate act of humility. The truth is, it is impossible to believe in God without experiencing humility; otherwise it would be a gross contradiction of perception. There are many whose spirits are lifted just by the thought that God exists, while deep within their souls they do not believe that He does. So, if we truly believe there is a God we don't have to go around trying to act humble; we are humble, and not from a position of weakness, but of strength. That is the source of humility. David was humble before God when he stood there with the slingshot in his hand; yet he was strong at the same time as he confronted the giant before him. Jesus was tender, loving and merciful, yet did not hesitate to pick up a whip and drive the money changers out of the temple.

There are some who cannot understand how a person can, with the choices of self-worth and humility, have it both ways. Yet we can truly have it both ways; we can have self-worth and humility at the same time. The combination of "Believe in God" and "Do unto others" makes room for them both. It would have been better for Paul to have emphasized the "Do unto others" message rather than trying to sell the "lowliness of mind" message.

Paul's "lowliness of mind" doctrine would have us all living as monks (With all due respect to monks). The teaching diminishes self-worth by setting up unnatural and consequential boundaries between brethren, making us victims of each other. Paul forgot that true humility is automatically experienced when we are in the presence of a powerful yet loving God; and it comes naturally…without practice.

ABOUT THE PATH TO SALVATION

Both Jesus and Paul taught a message of "salvation" and they are as different as daylight and dark. The thrust of Jesus' message was "repentance" and "the pursuit of righteousness" while Paul's message would have "faith and Grace" become a substitute for that repentance and pursuit of righteousness. At times you can't be a follower of Paul without denying Jesus. This is one of those times.

Jesus said the following in Luke 6 in describing the path to salvation:

> *²⁰ And he lifted up his eyes on his disciples, and said, Blessed be ye poor: for yours is the kingdom of God.²¹ Blessed are ye that hunger now: for ye shall be filled. Blessed are ye that weep now: for ye shall laugh.²² Blessed are ye, when men shall hate you, and when they shall separate you from their company, and shall reproach you, and cast out your name as evil, for the Son of man's sake.²³ Rejoice ye in that day, and leap for joy: for, behold, your reward is great in heaven: for in the like manner did their fathers unto the prophets.²⁴ But woe unto you that are rich! for ye*

have received your consolation.²⁵ Woe unto you that are full! for ye shall hunger. Woe unto you that laugh now! for ye shall mourn and weep.²⁶ Woe unto you, when all men shall speak well of you! for so did their fathers to the false prophets.²⁷ But I say unto you which hear, Love your enemies, do good to them which hate you,²⁸ Bless them that curse you, and pray for them which despitefully use you.²⁹ And unto him that smiteth thee on the one cheek offer also the other; and him that taketh away thy cloak forbid not to take thy coat also.³⁰ Give to every man that asketh of thee; and of him that taketh away thy goods ask them not again.³¹ And as ye would that men should do to you, do ye also to them likewise.³² For if ye love them which love you, what thank have ye? for sinners also love those that love them.³³ And if ye do good to them which do good to you, what thank have ye? for sinners also do even the same.³⁴ And if ye lend to them of whom ye hope to receive, what thank have ye? for sinners also lend to sinners, to receive as much again.³⁵ But love ye your enemies, and do good, and lend, hoping for nothing again; and your reward shall be great, and ye shall be the children of the Highest: for he is kind unto the unthankful and to the evil.³⁶ Be ye therefore merciful, as your Father also is merciful.³⁷ Judge not, and ye shall not be judged: condemn not, and ye shall not be condemned: forgive, and ye shall be forgiven:³⁸ Give, and it shall be given unto you; good measure, pressed down, and shaken together, and running over, shall men give into your bosom. For with the same measure that ye mete withal it shall be measured to you again.³⁹ And he spake a parable unto them, Can the blind lead the blind? shall they not both fall into the ditch?⁴⁰ The disciple is not above his master: but every one that is perfect shall be as his master.⁴¹ And why beholdest thou the mote that is in thy brother's eye, but perceivest not the beam that is in thine own eye?⁴² Either how canst thou say to thy brother, Brother, let me pull out the mote that is in thine eye, when thou thyself beholdest not the beam that is in thine own eye? Thou hypocrite, cast out first the beam out of thine own eye, and then shalt thou see clearly to pull out the mote that is in thy brother's eye.⁴³ For a good tree bringeth not forth corrupt fruit; neither doth a corrupt tree bring forth good fruit.⁴⁴ For every tree is known by his own fruit. For of thorns men do not gather figs, nor of a bramble bush gather they grapes.⁴⁵ A good man out of the good treasure of his heart bringeth forth that which is good; and an evil man out of the evil treasure of his heart bringeth forth that which is evil: for of the abundance of the heart his mouth speaketh.⁴⁶ And why call ye me, Lord, Lord, and do not the things which I say?⁴⁷ Whosoever cometh to me, and heareth my sayings, and doeth them, I will shew you to whom he is like:⁴⁸ He is like a man which built an house, and digged deep, and laid the foundation on a rock: and when the flood arose, the stream beat vehemently upon that house, and could not shake it: for it was founded upon a rock.⁴⁹ But he that heareth, and doeth not, is like a man that without a foundation built an house upon the earth; against which the stream did beat vehemently, and immediately it fell; and the ruin of that house was great.

You say all that sounds too complicated? OK, you may like the simplified version. Jesus simplified it on other occasions by reducing it to one sentence: "Do unto others as you would have them do unto you." That makes it uncomplicated; Hard to implement? Yes. Complicated? No.

Reading that detail of what Jesus taught, it becomes obvious He wasn't suggesting that we do good things just for the reward, rather from a truly generous and loving heart. That is the only basis that justifies our works before God. I reject the notion that a person must perform good works as if it were a job to be done for the wage of "salvation" and "Heaven". Our righteous works must be the natural result of a change of heart brought about by repentance. The works are done because as we learn about and then pursue the righteousness of God, we evolve toward God's righteousness as we become a child of God. That does not suggest we work for our salvation. Sincere repentance is at the heart of it all and actually believing it is truly God's message to us is the catalyst to make it all happen. The greatest difference about how some understand Jesus' teachings is that part where Jesus declares we are to be kind and generous to our enemies. Some may say that Jesus has never mentioned that to them in their discussions with Him. It's downright weird that His Spirit would never bring it to our attention because that's exactly where most of us fail the "love" test. On the other hand, although we are to be kind and generous to our enemies, that does not mean we are not to defend ourselves and our families from harm's way. David gave us an example of how to do that with his slingshot. There's nothing inconsistent with loving our enemy while at the same time not allowing him to devour us. That patterns after God's teachings.

The Disciple John went on to teach the salvation principle declared by Jesus when he said:

"And <u>hereby we do know that we know Him, if we keep His commandments</u>. He that saith "I know Him", and keepeth not his commandments, is a liar, and the truth is not in him. But whoso keepeth His word, in him verily is the love of God perfected: hereby know we that we are in Him. He that saith he abideth in Him ought himself also so to walk, even as He walked (1ˢᵗ John 2:3-6).

The thrust of Paul's message was divided between his treatment of "The Holy Spirit" and "God's grace." Jesus said the gate is narrow and few will enter in. Paul said the gate is wide open and we're all going through it. Paul's message has been carried forth by some elements of the Church Institution to this day while Jesus' message is pretty much ignored. Jesus was referring to the "gate" as being the gate to life. The church institution could be envisioning the "gate" as being the door to the church-house.

The following explanation of salvation by Paul pretty well summarizes everything he taught about it:

"But what saith it? "The word is nigh thee, even in thy mouth, and in thy heart:" that is, the word of <u>FAITH, which we preach</u>; That if thou shalt confess with thy mouth the Lord Jesus, and shalt believe in thine heart that God hath raised Him from the dead, thou shalt be saved." (Rom. 10:8-9)

In that declaration by Paul, "faith" and whatever feelings are in your "heart" replaces the salvation taught by Jesus as reported in the gospels of Matthew, Mark, Luke and John. Also compare Paul's "stand-alone" presentation of faith with what James taught about it in James 2: 14-18:

> *"What doth it profit, my brethren, though a man say he hath faith, and have not works? can faith save him? If a brother or sister be naked, and destitute of daily food, And one of you say unto them, Depart in peace, be ye warmed and filled; notwithstanding ye give them not those things which are needful to the body; what doth it profit? Even so faith, if it hath not works, is dead, being alone. Yea, a man may say, Thou hast faith, and I have works: shew me thy faith without thy works, and I will shew thee my faith by my works."*

Paul turned salvation's result primarily toward developing a personal relationship with Jesus' Spirit and publicly honoring the image of Jesus and His death and Paul pretty much downplays repentance or pursuing righteousness as being part of the deal. Consequently, today's practice of Christianity is almost totally defined as participating in "canned" religious services invented by the Church Institution. The Institution attempts to control the (1) why, (2) when, (3) where and (4) how that God and Jesus are to be worshipped. Based on their "Paulinian" doctrines they would lead us to believe that God is an unrepentant narcissist who created mankind only as a source of praise and worship to Himself. If that was true God would not be so much focused on us and our needs, wants and desires; yet scripture tells us that God is indeed focused on us and also that He expects more from us than a canned worship experience. Although God created man in His own likeness and image (Genesis 1) mankind fell short of God's likeness when he trashed the love part and Paul failed to emphasize that in some of his presentations of the biblical God-man relationship. When man threw-out the love part of God's likeness, God sent Jesus to try to put it back together, giving us choice to either accept or reject it.

Paul obviously ignored much of what Jesus taught because Paul was basically into promoting worship without repentance, which brings us up to date as multitudes gather to worship Jesus with little love in their heart toward anyone outside their circle of friends. In conformation of Paul's doctrines, many of our "clergy" are now reluctant to declare a position against most immorality existing in our culture. They would merely have you "rev-up" that personal relationship with Jesus while ignoring many of the virtues taught directly by Him as well as by God the Father in the "Old Testament." They teach us to "fall in love with Jesus" while ignoring everything He taught. As an example of what's out there, I recently heard the pastor of a prominent church in Flower Mound, Texas teach that the "forbidden fruit" is scripture itself, with all its old rules and it's do's and don'ts. That is right out of Paul's handbook and Paul taught what he taught in spite of the fact that some of Jesus' earlier teachings were the exact opposite to Paul's concepts. When you're dealing primarily with emotion you can get some people to follow you anywhere and multitudes now follow after a fantasy... a false Christ. One may rationalize the Jesus "love-fest" anyway they want, but when it excludes Jesus' teachings, it becomes a form of anti-Christ.

When Jesus talked to the "Woman at the well," there she asked him: "Should we go to Jerusalem to worship or should we worship in this mountain? (John 4:19-26)" Jesus replied: "You have no idea what you are worshiping. You don't have to go anywhere to worship. God is a Spirit and He seeks those to worship Him in Spirit and in a true doctrine." (Paraphrased) Jesus, of course, taught that true doctrine and we should listen to Jesus, not Paul. Although Paul "covered the bases" by also teaching repentance and pursuit of righteousness, that did not alter his other contradictory and explicit definitions of salvation, which excluded them.

Paul had a habit of first quoting sound doctrine (from Jesus or God), but then added other statements to it, both there and in other places, which would appear to compromise or deny the doctrine altogether. For example, the following is a key verse he wrote that deals with one of his definitions of salvation:

"For by grace are ye saved through faith; and that not of yourselves: It is the gift of God: Not of works, lest any man should boast. For we are His workmanship, created in Christ Jesus unto good works, which God hath before ordained that we should walk in them." (Eph. 2:8-10)

It appears that Paul was trying to cover all the bases here in a couple of sentences which resulted in some confusion that eventually led millions of followers to seek God's Spirit while turning away from scripture altogether. Although there is contradiction in what Paul said here, most of the confusion however comes when clergy omits the last sentence when they teach it. Paul would ultimately lead us directly to that "personal relationship with Jesus"…"Do not pass GO, Do not collect $200; run straight into the arms of Jesus." "Me and Jesus, we've got our own thing going" is the title of a song written in the 60's and recorded by George Jones and perfectly explains that point. If read carefully, Paul's statement does cover the bases; however, it comes across as a "yes you can-no you can't" statement that left the door wide open for the John Calvin's of the world to mess with. Rick Warren put the final touches on the "Me and Jesus" song but his emphasis is more on "Me" than "Jesus" and that's about where we are today.

Paul appeared to be double-talking in many other statements he made. As an example, in his letter to the Philippians he stated in the 2nd chapter, verse 6: *Who, being in the form of God, thought it not robbery to be equal with God.*" That statement can be read that Jesus was God or that Jesus was not God. Paul presented information in contradictory terms many times and as we apply multiple-choice in selecting from his "yes you can-no you can't" presentation of issues, we can choose not to pursue righteousness, rather just accept it as a wonderful gift from Jesus…no strings attached. God I love that man. Rock on.

Jesus was explicit in His declaration to Paul about what Paul's mission was to be. According to Paul himself, he was told the following by Jesus' Spirit:

> "*To open their eyes and to turn them from darkness to light, and from the power of Satan unto God, that they may receive forgiveness of sins.*" (Acts 26:18)

Jesus appears to be saying that a person should actually repent from not pattering their lives after God's simple rules, to intentionally learn about and then "<u>turn</u>" their concept of life toward the righteousness of God as being the entrance to salvation. Paul taught repentance but then went on to emphasize a reliance on "Grace" as the underlying source of that repentance and the catalyst of salvation itself. With Paul it had to be instantaneous and complete with no strings attached. That, of course, would make it impossible to actually repent. Paul's definition of "grace" would create repentance by proxy. This is not to minimize the grace factor; it's like which comes first the chicken or the egg. Paul evidently considered grace as being the chicken; yet it could be the egg, or even both.

It was Paul and Paul alone who wrote that Jesus spoke to him personally after He was crucified and resurrected and told him: "My grace is sufficient for thee." (2nd Cor. 12:9) That is the only place in scripture where Jesus is quoted as having ever spoken the word "grace." It was Paul that actually made that statement and it was Paul that gave it wings in his version of salvation, not Jesus. The statement, reported only by Paul, turned out to be the key underpinning of Paul's gospel. It enabled Paul to discount repentance and discount learning about and pursuing God's righteousness and totally paved the way for Paul's definition of spirituality. Here, Paul would have Jesus waiting 40 or so years after His death to redefine a salvation that is totally inconsistent with the "four gospels" presentations.

I do not want to minimize the wonderful word "Grace" because Jesus embodies Grace. When He spoke of Himself, however,

He spoke in more explicit terms. He spoke of Himself in the following ways: "I am your friend if you do what I tell you." "If you love me keep my commandments." "Why do you call me Lord...Lord and do not the things I say." (Paraphrased) A lot of folks have used Paul's definition of grace to nullify and make void those statements, as well as other things that Jesus said.

In a "which comes first-the chicken or the egg" scenario Paul is clearly unwilling to choose between grace and righteousness in some instances while leaning heavily toward grace in others. His confusing presentation of such a significant element of salvation's definition allowed John Calvin and many more after him to deny that grace and works are compatible and they went on to take the neurotic position that a person cannot regard their good works as being the result of salvation. They are afraid we might just feel a little pride by doing something constructive. They would have us not feel good about doing anything good. Keep that head down and those eyes closed (don't peek) as you perform good deeds and then believe that it was not you that actually did the deeds, but the Hoy Spirit. John Calvin took the position that no man is capable of personally choosing to do anything good; explaining that any such good work could only come as a miracle performed by The Holy Spirit independently working within that person. Calvin would have us not being able to get up in the morning, dress ourselves and tie our own shoes without a divine intervention by God. That raises the question of why the Bible teaches the many specifics of God's righteousness and then teaches us to pursue that righteousness if, according to Calvin, we are incapable of doing anything righteous. Make sense?

I have heard John 19:30 quoted many times where Jesus stated "It is finished" just before He died and was taught that Jesus was saying by that statement that His death, by itself, was to be the central and finished focus of our being forgiven by God which resulted in a completed salvation. We have been preached to and have heard songs sung proclaiming it, although on reflection it doesn't appear that is what Jesus meant at all when He said: "It is finished." Jesus had already made a very similar statement (John 17:4) just a short time before He was taken to hang there on the cross and seemed to be repeating it again at the end of His life. In the first instance, He was praying to God as His crucifixion was imminent and near when He said: *"I have glorified thee on the earth: **I have finished the work which thou gavest me to do**.*" Isn't it likely that Jesus' use of the phrase "It is finished" a short time later during his crucifixion was again referring to his mission on earth that He had prayed about just a short time before? He never taught that His death would be the "finished" work to gain salvation while he was living. Why would He be teaching such a thing in one last sentence with His last living breath? And what was the work Jesus was referring to in His prayer to God shortly before His crucifixion?

> *"I have given them thy word." (John 17:14), "Sanctify them through thy truth: **thy word is truth**." (John 17:17), **"To this end was I born, and for this cause came I into the world, that I should bear witness unto the truth." (John 18:37)***

That is Jesus' mission statement and there is nothing there that suggests that His martyrdom by itself was planned by God to become the principle element of one's salvation. It was Paul who taught that. Jesus' stated unequivocally that His life's mission was to teach God's righteousness and the shedding of His blood is no less significant if done for that alone. Although He obviously knew he was the Messiah and that scripture had prophesied well in advance that the Messiah would be killed, He nevertheless never said it was His mission to die; rather accepted death as being a consequence of carrying out His mission as well as the prophesies.

His teachings about God's righteousness and freedom from religion threatened to come between the thousands of people who were following Him and the religious leaders of that day. Jesus was a revolutionary with a mission to free people from man-made religions. In the practice of Christianity, He is still celebrated by many only because He died (as a substitute or offering to God for their sins) yet those same folks do not appear to have ever learned anything about the righteousness he died for.

The Apostle Peter, appointed by Jesus to build His church, clearly described the <u>sacrificial nature</u> of Jesus' death in 1st Peter 1:16-23:

> *16 Because it is written, Be ye holy; for I am holy.*

> *17 And if ye call on the Father, who without respect of persons judgeth according to every man's work, pass the time of your sojourning here in fear:*

¹⁸ Forasmuch as ye know that ye were not <u>redeemed</u> with corruptible things, as silver and gold, from your vain conversation received by tradition from your fathers;

¹⁹ <u>But with the precious blood of Christ, as of a lamb without blemish and without spot</u>:

²⁰ Who verily was foreordained before the foundation of the world, but was manifest in these last times for you,

²¹ <u>Who by him do believe in God</u>, that raised him up from the dead, and gave him glory; <u>that your faith and hope might be in God.</u>

²² <u>Seeing ye have purified your souls in obeying the truth through the Spirit unto unfeigned love of the brethren, see that ye love one another with a pure heart fervently</u>:

²³ <u>Being born again, not of corruptible seed, but of incorruptible, by the word of God, which liveth and abideth for ever.</u>

Peter is the rock that Jesus built His church on and there is nothing said here by Peter that would ever lead a person to believe that Jesus' death was intended by God to be a sacrificial substitute for repentance and the pursuit of righteousness. Peter clearly stated the case in its entirety. It was Paul that changed and distorted the true nature of Jesus' sacrificial death.

Jesus once said: "Why do you call me Lord while refusing to do the things that I have taught you." (Paraphrased) That practice of calling Jesus "Lord" in music or in chants is exactly what some Church Institutions emphasize to their congregations and that's pretty much everything that happens in their Christian experience during their entire lifetime. They do the same thing over and over weekend after weekend and don't seem to tire of it. They are content with the programmed emotional high they achieve at their church pep-rally once every week or so and consider that as being a fulfillment of everything Jesus requires of them. They are programmed to call Jesus "Lord, Lord" and are also programmed not to do anything he taught. Paul's emphasis of the "grace" factor has led multitudes to accept the principle that they cannot and will not learn about nor attempt to practice the righteousness Jesus came to teach us about. For them it continues to be: "Me and Jesus, we've got our own thing going."

About A Personal Relationship With Jesus

The dynamics of a personal relationship provide the greatest rewards that life has to offer. A "personal relationship" with Jesus can become even more heart-felt and real than any other relationship. So then, a personal relationship with Jesus is the ultimate experience. We are not here to dispute either the existence or the detail of any relationship, including a relationship with Jesus. However, logic begs the question of what a perceived "Jesus-relationship" consists of when it produces a lifestyle that contradicts most everything Jesus stood for. That is a legitimate question, is it not? If I am "off base" here, I wish someone would explain to me just how it works that a person can have that personal relationship while living their life completely opposed to most everything Jesus taught. I will offer an answer to my own question: Those issues could be the result of only one thing. Jesus' personality has been redefined by religious politicians to suit the folks. It would naturally follow that some of them have a "personal relationship" with a phantom spirit that was invented just for them. If it does not reflect or produce or influence hardly anything Jesus taught, then their spirit friend is likely not

Jesus' Spirit. What other conclusion can we come to? The deceit is accompanied and even encouraged by our ego. At times that powerful ego betrays our good intentions and with only the slightest bit of flattery we willingly surrender our common sense and all our principles just to accomplish trivial desires or praise.

There are many who are devoted to a belief that having that "personal relationship" eliminates a requirement for them to know about or attempt to practice the primary things that Jesus taught in scripture (The origin and only basis for Christianity). They have been programmed by their clergy to give priority to communicating with Jesus through a personal spiritual connection while downplaying or ignoring the need to also learn about and follow what Jesus taught in scripture. God and Jesus are being presented to us as being no more than another hi-tech "dot-com" gadget that we fully control. We not only have a "mute" button on our Jesus remote, we have a "delete" button as well. Initially we are taught to just "invite" Jesus to come into our heart and that invitation alone begins the relationship. We are encouraged to just invite Him in and start talking to Him and He will take it from there to manage our life for us as well as tell us everything we want to know about anything. It is said that talking with Him gets easier with practice. Their whole concept of Christianity appears to be just spiritually "hanging out" with Jesus and many go on from there to describe Jesus as being "awesome" and indeed He is. He's also cool. He's everything….I could not agree more. (I do not deny here that having a relationship with Jesus is legitimate, nor that talking to Him as well as hearing from Him is central to that relationship)

Although they are rarely taught, most clergy never openly deny the teachings by Jesus that are clearly in conflict with the way they promote spiritualization. They accomplish their objective by giving emphasis to spiritualization while ignoring most of scripture's standards concerning human relationships. This is a very sensitive subject to many people and I will attempt to tread softly here while not denying either logic or the truth (as I see it). When the congregations were turned away from scripture they were also turned away from foundational Christian ethics and we have to ask ourselves why a spiritual relationship with Jesus would not always produce some recognizable form of virtue or ethics in the way we see and do unto others. Jesus Himself said that we are His friends if we follow His teachings. Are we all talking about the same Jesus here? I personally attribute the Institutionalized Church and its practice of turning away from scripture for the ruin of our culture and the destruction of our nation as it was founded and I have addressed that conclusion throughout this writing and others.

There are now many who do not use the bible as their source for defining Christianity except for a few favorite excerpts still in their memory about God's love and kindness. It is likely their personal understanding about Jesus differs with many others in their group because those other people have also independently constructed their own relationships based on their own individual concepts about everything. At times we could find 500 folks meeting together to worship 500 different images of Jesus. Their common purpose comes from their belief that the man-God "Jesus" sacrificed his life for the specific purpose of establishing the way to salvation (Heb. 9:26) and that individual salvation is accomplished only by their acknowledgement of that death sacrifice along with their invitation to Jesus to come into their heart. With that in mind, it doesn't really matter that they all understand Jesus differently because it is their common belief concerning His death that brings uniformity to the group.

The Christian community that I come from can be described as a strange group because when we were together in an informal setting we almost never talked about or discussed scripture, God, Jesus, or anything else related to our religion. In fact, outside of church we went years without a single reference to the subject. One would occasionally hear another person comment (in church) about how "cool" or "awesome" Jesus was and you would most likely hear some of us pray to Him at mealtime thanking Him for our meals using informal buddy-buddy jargon as we asked Him for favors. None of those comments are intended to belittle their belief and practice. I grew up among them and speak of the practice from experience. There's not anything wrong or bad with any of that of course; my point being many people's "Christianity" is never addressed or even thought of except when they are in church. That is their Christianity and much of it is designed more toward social activities and entertainment than it is to authentic bible study.

I also have a personal relationship with Jesus; yet it is somewhat different than some I know about. Mine is based on both His Spirit as well as His written word. Some allow conflict between the two while I believe there should be uniformity. They believe to give scripture that kind of status would limit God's Spirit. To me, that would be denying that God's Spirit had anything to do with scripture. If it is from the same Spirit, should they not be compatible?

The building blocks and sequence to a relationship with God goes something like this: God said: *"Let us make man in our image, after our likeness: and let them have dominion over the fish of the sea, and over the fowl of the air, and over the cattle, and over all the earth, and over every creeping thing that creepeth upon the earth."* (Gen. 1) Then man turned his back on God and lived in rebellion to Him. Then God insisted that He is in charge when He said: *"For My thoughts are not your thoughts, neither are your ways My ways, saith the Lord. "For as the heavens are higher than the earth, so are My ways higher than your ways, and My thoughts than your thoughts."* (Isaiah 55:8-11). Then God followed that up by declaring: *"Behold, I set before you this day a blessing and a curse; A blessing, if ye obey the commandments of the Lord your God, which I command you this day: And a curse, if ye will not obey the commandments of the Lord your God."* (Deut. 11:26-27) Then Jesus finally said: *"If ye love me, keep my commandments."* (John 14:15) Jesus also said: *"You are my friend if you do everything I command you."*

The Apostle Paul's teachings have a lot to do with the way some have defined their thoughts about and/or relationship with God or Jesus. Forget what God and/or Jesus said about it, for many it's Paul that has defined (for them) just how it works.

Two examples of Paul's teachings which are somewhat different than the four gospels are as follows:

> *"Now we have received, not the spirit of the world, but the spirit which is of God; that we might know the things that are freely given to us of God. "Which things also we speak, not in the words which man's wisdom teacheth, but which the Holy Ghost teaches; comparing spiritual things with spiritual.* (1ˢᵗ Cor. 2:12-13)

> *"If Christ be in you, the body is dead because of sin; but the spirit is life because of righteousness. But if the Spirit of Him That raised up Jesus from the dead dwell in you, He That raised up Christ from the dead shall also quicken your mortal bodies by His Spirit that dwelleth in you. Therefore, brethren, we are debtors, not to the flesh, to live after the flesh. For if ye live after the flesh, ye shall die: but if ye through the Spirit do mortify the deeds of the body, ye shall live. For as many as are led by the Spirit of God, they are the sons of God. For ye have not received the Spirit of bondage again to fear; but ye have received the Spirit of adoption, whereby we cry, "Abba, Father." The Spirit itself beareth witness with our spirit, that we are the children of God."* (Rom. 8:8-16)

Although Paul taught we can rely on the feelings we get from our "spiritual relationship with God" to confirm our salvation, Jesus taught: *"Why do you call Me Lord, Lord and do not the things that I say."*

Then the Apostle John went on to teach:

> *"And <u>hereby we do know that we know Him, if we keep His commandments</u>. He that saith "I know Him", and keepeth not his commandments, is a liar, and the truth is not in him. But whoso keepeth His word, in him verily is the love of God perfected: hereby know we that we are in Him. He that saith he abideth in Him ought himself also so to walk, even as He walked."* (1ˢᵗ John 2:3-6).

Paul created confusion when his explanations about the function of God's Spirit differed so dramatically with other specific things Jesus and His disciples taught. Nothing that I have said here assumes that a personal relationship with God is not appropriate, nor does it insinuate that such relationship is void of feeling and emotion; far from it. It would merely make the point that we cannot totally separate the spirit from the flesh as Paul would have it; nor can we discount scripture that differs from Paul.

Acts 10:34 states: *"God is no respecter of persons."* To me that means we are all judged by the same rules.....God's rules; and we're not given individual and personal guidelines for our life based on our preconceived concepts about who or what God is. Original scripture does not say that God has a specific plan for each person's life. Scripture was re-written to make it say that. Jesus said He came to teach us everything God would have us know. He also said: "I have told you all things." So, our fundamental relationship with God is based on the standards He has already set which were confirmed by Jesus. That does not mean that God cannot or will not guide us by His Spirit in personal matters, but He has already told us "all things" which have application to all our concerns about life. Scripture says His Spirit will <u>remind</u> us of those things as we need to be reminded (John 14:26). Many will follow specific paths in life that they themselves create in their own minds while declaring them to be coming to them from God. (Read Jer.23:25-32)

Christianity, having become politically driven, has two different camps. The liberal camp prays to God for a new car and in time they acquire that new car and give God credit for it. The conservative camp earns and saves money and buys the car without praying for it. They don't feel like they are slighting God by not considering the car as being a miracle from God. They believe, as the bible states, that that's what naturally happens when people plan and work for something. The liberal camp, while acknowledging that work and saving the money is required, also believes it comes to them only as a miracle from God rather than from their own hard work. The liberal camp never read what King Solomon taught about that when he said:

> *"Eccl 2:24 There is nothing better for a man, than that he should eat and drink, and that he should make his soul enjoy good in his labour, This also I saw, that it was from the hand of God,"* and *"Eccl. 3:13 And also that every man should eat and drink, and enjoy the good of all his labour, it is the gift of God."*

Solomon was saying that it is through God's gift of life that we can labor to acquire our needs and wants to enjoy.

For some, to mentally or spiritually "hook-up" with God is nothing more than their creating their own personalized God as they imagine Him to be. They have theoretically achieved such a close relationship with their God that He allows them to frame only those questions they want God to address: "God, never mind what you have already written for mankind, I will ask you exactly what I want to know from you." In other words some would limit what God has to say to whatever it is they want to hear. Having presumably achieved that kind of "personal relationship," they go on to discount or ignore most of the basic biblical standards declared by God, claiming that they have now become irrelevant to them personally. That kind of influence over God allows them to virtually create a God of their choosing. In a "personal relationship" scenario, if man sets the agenda, does he not automatically become his own God by default? When he chooses and controls the subject matter in all of his conversations with God is he not talking to and answering himself? No wonder some publicly praise God with such fervor. They're actually praising themselves because they have created God in their own image. When many so-called Christians individually determine who God is and individually determine right and wrong and individually define ethics and individually define virtue, then the group no longer has a unified identity and its influence is diluted or lost on the world stage. United under one Biblical God we stand, divided we fall. Did anyone hear the crash?

With their personal hook-up they then get into "stuff" like: "God... should we go to Italy or France on vacation"...... "Thank you Jesus, I've always wanted to see Italy." They, in effect, have exchanged the simple principles that the real Jesus taught for something akin to a virtual emotion-driven religious model (Genie) designed by the church "Institution," and by doing so, assumed total and absolute authority over their Jesus.

Based on comments I have made over time there have been those who have asked me: "Don't you believe we're to achieve a personal relationship with Jesus?" My answer is: "Of course I do." On the other hand there are many different interpretations of just how that is done. Many will sing: "I am a friend of God....He calls me friend" and have never been told there are conditions for that friendship. I didn't say that...Jesus did.

The word "unconditional" is widely misused because the word (or its equivalent) does not appear in scripture. Some church institutions have over-used the word, hoping that it will come to define their membership's allegiance to the institution. Paul's spirituality thesis led to creation of the word "unconditional" as well as the details of how a personal relationship with God or Jesus actually functions. Some, in mentally developing that personal relationship will routinely consult God about which item to choose on a restaurant menu or even ask for God's opinion about whether to choose butter or margarine. A good answer from God would be: "When I created you I gave you dominion over the earth and everything in it and that includes the cow. Why don't you and the cow work it out?"

I wrote about some of my thoughts and impressions about the God/man relationship in my book <u>"A View from the Pew"</u> as follows: "I believe that prayer is precious. When a person becomes conscious of God's presence; that consciousness, alone, places them in a prayer mode. God's telephone to us has rung. We have lifted the receiver and placed it to our ear. It is then as if two people are sitting or walking silently and intentionally together, without conversation and with an open communication present between them; between us and God's Spirit. It is an acute awareness of God's presence that is in place here and a person doesn't have to actually pray in order to be consumed by that presence. Our thoughts alone toward Him automatically bring us into God's presence and His Spirit is no less distant from us when we are spiritually in His presence than it is when we verbally express prayer"

When my thoughts turn toward God and that "relationship," they are more about his written word (His advice and His promises) than about the emotion of a song or about religious programs or about touchdowns or restaurant menus and it's also more about spiritual things than about the physical things that I may want or need. Just remember: We can have that personal relationship with Jesus without following Paul's concepts.

You say you by-passed all that "malarkey" and went straight to the man? I say: "good for you." Maybe you can put in a good word for me.

ABOUT THE PURSUIT OF RIGHTEOUSNESS

"He leadeth me in the paths of righteousness for His name's sake" (Excerpt from 23rd Psalms)

There are some who skip that part of the 23rd Psalms. They mentally gravitate to the "feel good" part of it that goes: "Surely goodness and mercy shall follow me all the days of my life, and I will dwell in the house of the Lord forever." Just leave out the righteousness part and they're good to go. That, of course, is also what they are being taught by many churches.

On numerous occasions Jesus re-emphasized that His followers were expected to learn about and pursue God's righteousness. Jesus declared that He was born just to bring us that message. The following quotes from Jesus merely scratch the surface of the many times He taught the pursuit of righteousness:

➤ *"I have given them thy word." (John 17:14), "Sanctify them through thy truth: thy word is truth." (John 17:17), "To this end was I born, and for this cause came I into the world, that I should bear witness unto the truth." (John 18:37)*

➤ *"If you continue in My word, then you are My disciples indeed; and you shall know the truth, and the truth shall make you free.…..If the Son therefore shall make you free, you shall be free indeed." (John 8:31-32 & 36)*

➤ *"Therefore all things whatsoever ye would that men should do to you, do ye even so to them: for this is the law and the prophets. Enter ye in at the strait gate; for wide is the gate, and broad is the way, that leadeth to destruction, and many there be which go in thereat. Because strait is the gate, and narrow is the way, which leadeth unto life, and few there be that find it. Beware of false prophets, which come to you in sheep's clothing, but inwardly they are ravening wolves. Ye shall know them by their fruits. Do men gather grapes of thorns, or figs of thistles? Even so every good tree bringeth forth good fruit; but a corrupt tree bringeth forth evil fruit. A good tree can not bring forth evil fruit, neither can a corrupt tree bring forth good fruit. Every tree that bringeth not forth good fruit is hewn down, and cast into the fire. Wherefore by their fruits ye shall know them. Not every one that sayeth unto Me, "Lord, Lord", shall enter into the kingdom of heaven; BUT HE THAT DOETH THE WILL OF MY FATHER WHICH IS IN HEAVEN. Many will say to Me in that day, "Lord, Lord, have we not prophesied in Thy name? and in Thy name have cast out devils? And in Thy name done many wonderful works?" And then will I profess unto them, "I never knew you: depart from Me, ye that work iniquity." (Mat. 7:12-23)*

➤ ***"He that hath My commandments, and keepeth them, he it is that loveth Me;*** *and he that loveth Me shall be loved* *of My father, and I will love him, and will manifest Myself to him." Judas saith unto Him, not Iscariot, "Lord, how is it that thou wilt manifest thyself* **unto us**, *and not unto the world?" Jesus answered and said unto him, "If a man love Me, he will keep my words: and My Father will love him, and We will come unto him, and make Our abode with him. He that loveth Me not keepeth not My sayings: and the word which ye hear is not Mine, but the Father's Which sent Me. These things have I spoken unto you, being yet present with you. But the Comforter, Which is the Holy Ghost, Whom the Father will send in My name, He will teach you all things, and bring all things to your remembrance, whatsoever I have said unto you." (John 14:21-26)*

➤ *"Yea, rather, blessed are they that hear the word of God, and keep it." And when the people were gathered thick together, He began to say, "This is an evil generation: they seek a sign; and there shall no sign be given it, but the sign of Jonas the prophet." (Luke 11:28-29)*

➤ *Then said one unto Him, "Lord, are there few that be saved?" And He said unto them, "Strive to enter in at the strait gate: for many, I say unto you, will seek to enter in, and shall not be able. When once the master of the house is risen up, and hath shut the door, and ye begin to stand without, and to knock at the door, saying, 'Lord, Lord, open unto us;' and He shall answer and say unto you, I know ye not whence ye are: Then shall ye begin to say, 'We have eaten and drunk in thy presence, and Thou hast taught in our streets.' But He shall say, 'I tell you I know you not whence ye are; depart from Me, all ye workers of iniquity.'" (Luke 13:23-27)*

➤ *"If ye keep My commandments, ye shall abide in My love. Ye are My friends, IF ye do whatsoever I command you." (John 15:10&14)*

➤ *"And he said unto him, "Why callest thou me good? There is none good but one, that is, God: but if thou will enter into life, keep the commandments." He saith unto him, which? Jesus said, "Thou shalt do no murder, Thou shalt not commit adultry, Thou shalt not steal, Thou shalt not bear false witness, Honor thy father and thy mother: and, Thou shalt love thy neighbor as thyself." (Mat. 19:17-19)*

➤ *"For a good tree bringeth not forth corrupt fruit: neither doth a corrupt tree brng forth good fruit. For every tree is known by his own fruit. For of thorns men do not gather figs, nor of a bramble bush gather they grapes. A good man out of the good treasure of his heart bringeth forth that which is good; and an evil man out of the evil treasure of his heart bringeth forth that which is evil: for of the abundance of the heart his mouth speaketh. And why call ye Me, Lord, Lord, and do not the things which I say? Whosoever cometh to Me, and heareth My sayings, AND DOETH THEM, I will shew you to whom he is like: He is like a man which built an house, and digged deep, and laid the foundation on a rock: and when the flood arose, the stream beat vehemently upon that house, and could not shake it: for it was founded upon a rock. But he that heareth and doeth not, is like a man that without a foundation built a house upon the earth; against which the stream did beat vehemently, and immediately it fell; and the ruin of that house was great." (Luke 6:43-49)*

Many have concluded they don't care what Jesus may have taught about pursuing righteousness. They obviously have come to believe what they have been taught about it and seem to be comfortable that their perceived personal hook-up with Jesus does not then require them to actually be concerned about anything else He taught. The following is what the Apostle John also said about pursuing righteousness and John clearly answers the question here of "How one knows if they are truly 'born again'."

"And <u>hereby we do know that we know Him, if we keep His commandments</u>. He that saith "I know Him", and keepeth not his commandments, is a liar, and the truth is not in him. whoso keepeth His word, in him verily is the love of God perfected: hereby know we that we are in Him. He that saith he abideth in Him ought himself also so to walk, even as He walked (1ˢᵗ John 2:3-6).

Paul, on the other hand summarized his own inability to gain any righteousness as follows:

"For we know that the law is spiritual: but I am carnal, sold under sin. For that which I do I allow not: for what I would, that do I not; but what I hate, that do I. If then I do that which I would not, I consent unto the law that it is good. Now then it is no more I that do it, but sin that dwelleth in me. For I know that in me (that is, in my

flesh,) dwelleth no good thing: for to will is present with me; but how to perform that which is good I find not. For the good that I would I do not: but the evil which I would not, that I do. Now if I do that I would not, it is no more I that do it, but sin that dwelleth in me. I find then a law, that, when I would do good, evil is present with me. For I delight in the law of God after the inward man: But I see another law in my members, warring against the law of my mind, and bringing me into captivity to the law of sin which is in my members. O wretched man that I am! who shall deliver me from the body of this death? I thank God through Jesus Christ our Lord. So then with the mind I myself serve the law of God; but with the flesh the law of sin. (Romans 7:14-25)

In spite that Paul taught that he or we could not overtake the human instinct "to sin." Jesus taught; "Strive to enter in at the strait gate: for many, I say unto you, will seek to enter in, and shall not be able." (Luke 13:24) Jesus admonished us to "strive." Paul said forget it…you can't do it. Jesus also taught:"Be ye therefore perfect, even as you're Father which is in heaven is perfect." Jesus taught us to try to emulate God's righteousness. Paul said forget it…no way Hosea.

When Paul completely separated the actions of one's flesh from the influence of their own will, I see that as a declaration that he could have it both ways (unrighteousness equally alongside righteousness) and went on to set it as a pattern for others to follow. That was not what Jesus taught.

In summary, Jesus said: "Be ye righteous," and Paul said categorically: "No you can't." Paul said that as long as he wished not to sin that's all that counted because he would not be able to overcome sin. In spite of what Paul said in this instance, and taking into full account everything else the Bible teaches about the pursuit of righteousness (even from Paul himself), how could it ever be concluded that God will credit a person as having Jesus' righteousness without that person ever knowing anything about it or ever attempting to practice it? Such widespread misunderstanding came from Paul and not from Jesus.

ABOUT JESUS' MISSION

Jesus is quoted by the Disciple John as follows:

"God so loved the world, that he gave his only begotten Son, that whosoever believes in him should not perish, but have everlasting life. For God sent not his Son into the world to condemn the world; but that the world through him might be saved. He that believes on him is not condemned: but he that believes not is condemned already, because he has not believed in the name of the only begotten Son of God. And this is the condemnation, that light is come into the world, and men loved darkness rather than light, because their deeds were evil. For every one that doeth evil hates the light, neither cometh to the light, lest his deeds should be reproved. But he that doeth truth cometh to the light that his deeds may be made manifest, that they are wrought in God." (John 3:16-21)

The thrust of what is said here was changed by Paul who taught that Jesus' primary mission was to die a sacrificial death, which, when acknowledged by us, would become our substitute for repentance and righteous living. Is that not the opposite of what Jesus is teaching here?

Contrary to what Paul taught, Jesus specifically described his (Jesus') mission as follows:

> *"I have given them thy word." (John 17:14), "Sanctify them through thy truth: **thy word is truth**." (John 17:17), **"To this end was I born, and for this cause came I into the world, that I should bear witness unto the truth." (John 18:37)***

You say you've been going to "Church" 50 years and were never taught about Jesus' personal and very specific description of His mission? "Son-of-a-gun"... could that be because it conflicts with what Paul taught? Paul, on the other hand maintained in the book of Hebrews and other places that Jesus primary mission was to die in order that His death would become a sacrificial substitute for repentance and we are to believe that that alone will result in God's forgiving of our past, present and future sins, while our life goes on indistinguishable from the crowd. Jesus' death, then, became the catalyst of the Institutionalized Church going forward, while the real purpose of His declared mission was ignored. Also, read Luke's reporting of John's preparing the way for Jesus in Luke 1:68-80. Theirs (John the Baptist and Jesus) was all about teaching people to pursue God's righteousness as a way of life. That's what "conversion" means and it's something more than just a spiritual "hook-up." The spiritual "hook-up" is the natural fruit conversion will bear. It's an evolutionary process with conversion coming before the "hook-up."

In spite of Jesus' own declared mission, Paul changed it when he wrote:

"But we see <u>Jesus, who was made a little lower than the angles for the suffering of death</u>, crowned with glory and honour; <u>that he by the grace of God should taste death for every man</u>." (Heb. 2:9)

"He appeared to put away sin by the sacrifice of himself." (Heb. 9:26)

"Be ye therefore followers of God, as dear children; And walk in love, as Christ also hath loved us, <u>and hath given himself for us an offering and a sacrifice to God</u> for a sweet smelling savour." (Eph. 5:2) [4]

Paul went on to "double-talk" his permissive approach to the issue of "righteous living" in the 3RD through the 10th chapters of the book of Romans, claiming there that Jesus death was planned by God as being a sacrifice that we may substitute for the pursuit of righteous living. There, Paul went all the way back to Abraham to establish that "faith" was itself "righteousness." The content of the 8 chapters in the book of Romans is too large to reproduce in this writing but should be read by those having an interest in the details of Paul's thesis on the subject. He explains just how one is perceived as being righteous without ever being righteous. It sounds really neat but I can't find where Jesus ever taught that kind of spookiness. Jesus rather taught repentance and pursuit of righteous living. The Apostle John stated it very well in 1st

John 3:7 when he said: *"Little children, let no man deceive you: he that doeth righteousness is righteous, even as he is righteous."*

Paul's theme in growing the early "Christian" movement remains a theme in the presentation of Christianity today. In fact, today (1/20/13) I heard the pastor of a prominent local church in Flower Mound Texas teach that the main job of the Holy Spirit is to teach us that we are righteous. He made that remarkable declaration even though it is not contained in the bible. He quickly flipped through the Bible selecting little excerpts out of their context here and there insinuating that he had justified it by scripture. He would also read a line or two having nothing to do with it then expand it through his own interpretation to make his point. Those followers of Paul that keep pointing to the "Grace" factor as an excuse not to attempt the practice of righteous living always ignore the next sentence following the scripture they rely on:

> *"For by grace are ye saved through faith; and that not of yourselves: It is the gift of God: Not of works, lest any man should boast. <u>For we are His workmanship, created in ChristJesus UNTO good works, which God hath before ordained that **we should walk in them**</u>. (Eph. 2:8-10)*

Paul never hesitated to teach it both ways.

Jesus died (was taken forcibly by religious leaders and then executed by the government) because He was bringing God's truth to a selfish world and to that extent He died for our sins. However, Jesus didn't say it was His mission to die, nor was it stated anywhere in the Old Testament or in the four gospels that it was His mission to die; Paul did. Paul taught that the resurrected Jesus completely changed the mission that He had just earlier declared to Pilate. On that occasion, Jesus specifically identified His mission which was "to bear witness to (God's) truth," and was to be the only purpose for his life. How did Paul get away with that?

Jesus had insight of His impending death and He expressed it to His Disciples in Matthew 20:18-19:

> *"Behold, we go up to Jerusalem; and the Son of man shall be betrayed unto the chief priests and unto the scribes, and they shall condemn him to death, And shall deliver him to the Gentiles to mock, and to scourge, and to crucify him: and the third day he shall rise again."*

Jesus, being well aware that He, being the Messiah, would be killed as spoken by the prophets, confirmed His advanced knowledge of His death as follows:

> *"Likewise (He) also (passed) the cup after supper, saying, This cup is the new testament in my blood, which is shed for you." And truly the Son of man goeth, as it was determined. (Luke 22:20 & 22)*

> Mat.26:28 version: *"For this is my blood of the new testament, which is shed for many for the remission of sins."*

> *"But all this was done, that the scriptures of the prophets might be fulfilled. Then all the disciples forsook him, and fled." (Mat. 26:56)*

Just because Jesus knew He would be killed did not make that His mission; rather He was willing to die if necessary in order to carry out that mission. He prayed to God the Father that if possible the "cup" would pass from Him because He was exceedingly sorry that He was facing death (Mat. 26 and Mark 14). His death and resurrection, along with the accomplishment of the fulfillment of scripture, demonstrated to the multitudes that He was truly The Son of God. Yet, nothing happened before or after His death and resurrection to contradict what He Himself had declared to be His mission. That would lead one to conclude He was killed specifically to stop Him from carrying out that mission.

His resurrection, added to His miracles, together proved that He was sent by God. They together gave credibility to everything He had taught. There is a significant distinction between that conclusion and Paul's teaching that His death was planned by God to become a sacrificial substitute for the "past" as well as "future" sins of mankind. Paul's versions resulted in the Christian community coming to praise and honor His death while ignoring His mission. Jesus taught repentance and to truthfully honor His death is to adopt and pursue the standards He taught. Unfortunately, many praise Him with mounting and intensified fervor and pay little or no attention to what He taught.

ABOUT PRAYER

Most everything I was originally taught about praying originated with the "Apostle" Paul and when it comes to praying, Paul taught the opposite to everything Jesus taught about it.

At a point in their relationship, because Jesus had apparently not taught His Disciples about praying; nor had emphasized up to that point that they should pray at all, they said to Him: *"Lord, teach us to pray."* Here is an account of the incident:

> *"And it came to pass, that, as he was praying in a certain place, when he ceased, one of his disciples said unto him, Lord, teach us to pray, as John also taught his disciples. And he said unto them, When ye pray, say, Our Father which art in heaven, Hallowed be thy name. Thy kingdom come; Thy will be done, as in heaven, so in earth. Give us day by day our daily bread. And forgive us our sins; for we also forgive every one that is indebted to us. And lead us not into temptation; but deliver us from evil." (Luke 11:1-4)*

Jesus continued His teaching:

"And when you pray, don't be like the hypocrites are: for they love to pray standing in the synagogues and in the corners of the streets, that they may be seen of men. Verily I say unto you, they have their reward. But when you pray, enter into your closet, and when you have shut your door, pray to the Father in secret; and your Father shall reward you openly. When you pray, don't use vain repetition as the heathen do for they think that they shall be heard for their much speaking. Don't be like them for your Father knows what things you have need of, before you ask him." (Mat. 6: 5-13)

Paul, on the other hand taught:

"Pray without ceasing; in everything give thanks: for this is the will of God in Christ Jesus concerning you." (1Thes. 5:17-18)

"Be careful for nothing; but in everything by prayer and supplication with thanksgiving let your requests be made known unto God." (Phil. 4:6)

exhort therefore that first of all, supplications, prayers, intercession, and giving of thanks be made for all men." (1st Tim. 2:1)

"Wherefore take unto you the whole armour of God......Praying always with all prayer and supplication in the Spirit, and watching thereunto with all perseverance and supplication for all saints (Eph. 6:13 and 18).

Paul evidently created those praying rules in order to establish prayer as a ritual; a ritual that was central to support the basic characteristics of the way he defined and organized the church and its practice of Christianity. Paul saw prayer as being the central focus of spirituality and although Jesus declared that total freedom comes from following scripture, Paul moved away from scripture and his emphasis toward spirituality allowed him greater input of his own doctrines rather than having to follow scripture's more specific standards. He obviously believed that promoting (artificially accelerating) the God/man interaction was more in keeping with his religious theories and objectives and he went on to promote much praying about everything. Ritualistic praying was promoted by Paul in order that we acquire God's instructions on a real-time basis and was to replace the use of scripture for our life pattern. So, in general, he led people toward a personalized approach to spirituality which included daily praying and listening for God's perceived voice or observing His perceived signs; which in-turn led them away from the Jesus "Do unto others" doctrine to what I describe as a "You and Jesus get your heads together and work it out between yourselves" doctrine. (No, I'm not against praying...just pray as Jesus taught.)

In addition to Jesus' opposite comments about prayer, other significant Bible characters differed dramatically with Paul's teachings. To paraphrase Solomon in Eccl. 5:2-3: <u>Don't be so hasty about how you pray to God to give you things because a person is intended to accomplish a goal by working for it; not foolishly asking God over and over for it.</u> *("Be not rash with thy mouth, and let not thine heart be hasty to utter anything before God. For God is in heaven, and thou upon earth: therefore let thy words be few. For a dream cometh through the multitude of business; and a fool's voice is known by multitude of words.")*

It is not my intention here to judge the pros and cons of how often we should pray and what we should pray for, rather to address the specifics that Jesus taught about it as compared to those of Paul and "let the cards fall where they may." Jesus taught that when we pray, we should pray directly to God the Father (not to Him). Paul began most of his letters to his churches with a prayer. Jesus did not routinely pray when he was speaking to followers; He just began speaking and did not begin or end His speaking with a prayer as did Paul. Most of His prayers were done in private settings, just as He taught.

When I am in the audience of a church service I personally prefer to hear a prayer spoken without background music. For me, that adds an element of theatrics to the praying that turns it into a stunt or a soap-opera. Is the music intended for me or for God? I wonder what God thinks about the background music. Generally speaking, the majority of church groups teach that a daily and progressive "prayer life" (as they call it) is essential in the <u>development</u> of that "personal spiritual relationship" with Jesus. Along with that they emphasize we should pray for those things we want or need and continue praying for them until we get them; and if and when we get what we prayed for, don't forget….it comes to us only because of a miracle performed by God and is no less significant a miracle than the resurrection. If we do not get what we prayed for in a reasonable time-frame then we are to conclude that God has decided that we either don't need it or else He has something better in mind for us down the road. At times, that creates the dilemma of having to guess whether or not God has rejected our prayer out-of-hand or is still thinking about it. The only thing they can tell us about that is that God cannot be rushed and cite history where praying went on for 40-50 years before God answered a specific prayer. I have noticed that some of those folks that pray for everything are pretty sneaky about how they will hedge on their expectation that God will actually answer their prayers. They will pray fervently for a Cadillac car (as example) and will end their praying by saying something like: "But not my will but Thine be done." They have covered their bases so that in their minds God is perceived to have answered their prayer by just saying no…you can't have it. I have watched many in the so-called Christian community sit on their hands and pray endlessly for the last 50 years for their personal wants and needs as well as for their government's well being while both of those concerns "went to hell in a hand basket." Jesus had it right. King Solomon had it right. Paul had it wrong.

Following after Paul, today's Christian culture prays endlessly for stuff. It is shameful how clergy misuses scripture to promote that practice. They refer us to James 4:2 reminding us that "we have not… because we ask not." If one wants to have insight into how we're being manipulated, go to the book of James and read the entire 3rd and 4th chapters and observe how they incredibly removed and quoted only part of a sentence completely out of its context to create the deception that all we have to do is pray for it and we've got it. Believing that could lead a person to imagine that many routine happenings in their life are actually miracles being performed for them by God.

In the first 5 chapters of the book of Ecclesiastes Solomon made some remarkable statements about how God makes provision for our needs and it did not involve praying for them. The characteristics of God's creation along with His specific instructions about how we are to conduct our lives are collectively designed by Him to produce successful outcomes and it requires no praying to achieve it. Also, the bible teaches that the natural goodness that comes to us from this earth falls on both the just and the unjust (He makes His rain to rain and sun to shine on the just and the unjust). It then naturally follows that a bad person can succeed in accomplishing wealth the same as a good person. That is not to say that some bad people don't achieve all or part of their success in an unscrupulous manner; however a person can be rotten to the core and still succeed by intelligent hard work. That same rule is intended to work for believers as well. Some become puzzled and wonder why God allows an evil person to prosper while others who are good, kind and generous struggle their entire lifetime. That's because they don't know everything scripture teaches about it. They appear to evaluate scripture and God only in physical and/or human emotional terms and never discover the uniqueness of the quite different Spirit of God. An evil person can legitimately prosper the same as anyone else. It's a universal rule that is all about sowing and reaping and applies to unbelievers as well as believers. So, we should do what Solomon advised. Quit praying for what we want or need and start working to accomplish it. According to Solomon, that is the principal method God uses to give us gifts. So, we need to get off our "buttocks" and help God out. That will make it more likely our prayer will be answered.

Bringing it all up to date, what King Solomon was telling us is that if we want to score a touchdown, hit a home run, make a lot of money, or find that special companion, we more than likely are going to have to get it done all by ourselves. We are God's instruments to achieve our own goals and He gave us His rules to help make it happen. I believe that <u>some</u> people who habitually go around publicly "thanking Jesus" for this that and the other are doing so merely to call attention to themselves. There are some who define that as "witnessing." They just want you to know how much God does for them <u>personally</u> and, of course, the presumption is that it's all deserved.

Here are some quotations from Solomon:

> *"There is nothing better for a man, than that he should eat and drink, and that he should make his soul enjoy good in his labour. This also I saw, that it was from the hand of God."*

> *"And also that every man should eat and drink, and enjoy the good of all his labour, it is the gift of God."*

> *"Wherefore I perceive that there is nothing better, than that a man should rejoice in his own works; for that is his portion"*

"Moreover the profit of the earth is for all: the king himself is served by the field."

"Behold that which I have seen: it is good and comely for one to eat and to drink, and to enjoy the good of all his labour that he taketh under the sun all the days of his life, which God giveth him: for it is his portion."

"Every man also to whom God hath given riches and wealth, and hath given him power to eat thereof, and to take his portion, and to rejoice in his labour; this is the gift of God."

Also, Psalms 128 declares:

"Walk after God and you will eat the labor of your hands."

Praying for "stuff" is emphasized by some clergy as being more important than knowing and understanding God's instructions already given to us about how we are to live our lives. Some lead us to believe that praying becomes an optional way to get the "stuff" we want or need, which only reinforces their natural instinct that "getting stuff" is what life is all about. If you don't think that is true just check out the fruit hanging-out there in their pews. Most everything outside of their "church-house" gatherings is all about getting stuff for their selves while giving little or no thought to "Doing for others." They could at least make an effort to be nice to folks. In the meantime, do clergy themselves appear to be (perhaps subconsciously) taking at least partial credit for everything good that praying supposedly brings our way? Some clergy appear to consider themselves as being a stand-in for God and assume too much of God's power as well as honor to themselves. Whether that is or is not a fair assessment of their assumed role, we can say for sure that prayer is being promoted by them as being a key ingredient to learning about and practicing Christianity while intentionally downplaying what Jesus taught about repentance and pursuing righteousness.

God can and will do anything He chooses including answering any prayer that comes to Him and at any time He chooses. We have allowed the praying concept to become commercialized because we seldom look to scripture to learn everything taught about it. Speaking of praying, I once wondered why Job didn't experience an intercession from God on his behalf when all those calamities were happening to him. Then when I began to read for myself I was reminded that God had told Satan he could have his way with Job as long as he didn't take his life. Could it be that the book of Job has a prominent place in scripture to teach us that God does not always intervene in a person's life affairs and yet that is no reason to turn our backs on God? He rather allows us to choose and pursue a life of our choice; a life that He has not planned in advance for us. Some folks eagerly accept the teaching that God indeed dictates or allows all of the events in their lives, including their death. Scripture was changed to make it say that because it can become a seductive philosophy to some by not having to assume any responsibility for their life, with it being designed in advance to be implemented by God Himself. Rock on.

I wonder if Paul ever read about Job and if he ever read what Solomon wrote in the book of Ecclesiastes about how God provides for us. Also, why are there so many "choices" defined for us in the Bible if we are not given the liberty to choose between them? God told us in scripture: "I have set before you life and death, blessing and cursing: Therefore, choose life that thou and thy seed may live" (Deut. 30:19-20). Does that sound like God gives us personal choice that will influence our destiny? Influencing our own outcome would eliminate our need to pray for "stuff" because according to King Solomon the most significant way God provides for our needs is through our own work.

Although it doesn't happen often, I'm not overly enthusiastic to be summoned to participate in verbal praying when the objective is to just have a group "chit-chat" with God. I don't want to be thought of as being a heathen just by resisting becoming a "prayer-partner" but it's hard avoiding that label to those that pray as a ritual. Routine praying, for them, has become such a significant part of their perceived Christian life and experience they become offended by the slightest reluctance to pray with them. It's like: "How dare you not want to pray. You, a Christian, and don't want to pray?" I believe how many times a person prays, when they pray and what they pray for should be a spontaneous thing determined independently by each individual and should not be promoted as a mandatory ritual by organized churches or even by individuals. I will also add that there are occasions when I fully endorse and embrace praying with another person or persons for specific reasons. On the other hand, I see praying has having become rather frivolous in the way it is sometimes now promoted. I have sat-in and participated in praying with others that turned out to be pray-a-thons with the interaction appearing to be just between the people present. I sensed that God was not in attendance. That kind of praying is what Paul taught and I simply prefer to follow Jesus teaching on the matter….not Paul. It is very difficult for someone in the praying culture to accept any practice other than their own. It's just hard to change one's mind about something as personal and sensitive as praying can become. My conclusion is: I am not offended by anyone's prayer habits and I hope they are not offended by mine.

A Summary
Of The Issue

Many of us were taught that Paul was selected by Jesus to establish and organize His church. We may not have been taught that Paul was specifically "commissioned" to organize the church, but most of our understanding about Christianity had its origin with Paul's teachings and we just assumed that what we were being taught was coming indirectly from Jesus through Paul. If one reads the entire bible with interest they will find that Jesus only had one message and it was identical for the Jews and the "Gentiles" alike (See "About Jesus' Mission"… herein). Even so, Paul did not teach that message. Paul assumed authority to change Jesus' doctrines to reflect his (Paul's) own concepts and along the way we came to accept Paul's teachings as being endorsed by Jesus Himself. Not once did we ever consider it anything but Jesus doctrine.

Paul never met Jesus while Jesus walked the earth and although Jesus never said that He expected Paul to do any such thing, Paul built an institution around many of his personal concepts and proclaimed it to be the church of Jesus Christ. Some of Paul's doctrine was written 67 years after

Jesus' crucifixion; and everything he wrote obviously came either from Jesus' Spirit or from his own mind. Relying on scripture only, this is what Jesus said (before His crucifixion) about building His church and He said it to The Apostle Peter, not Paul:

> *"15 He saith unto them, But whom say ye that I am?16 And Simon Peter answer ed and said, Thou art the Christ, the Son of the living God.17 And Jesus answered and said unto him, Blessed art thou, Simon Barjona: for flesh and blood hath not revealed it unto thee, but my Father which is in heaven.18 **And I say also unto thee, That thou art Peter, and upon this rock I will build my church**; and the gates of hell shall not prevail against it.19 And I will give unto thee the keys of the kingdom of heaven: and whatsoever thou shalt bind on earth shall be bound in heaven: and whatsoever thou shalt loose on earth shall be loosed in heaven." (Mat.16)*

The statement by Jesus: "Upon this rock I will build my church" was so profound it had to be acknowledged, even by those clergy who taught us to follow after Paul. As I recall, it was presented to us in a totally abstract manner by refocusing our attention only on Peter's statement: "Thou art the Christ, the son of the living God." They taught us that that statement alone was to be the principle (or the "rock") that Jesus was addressing and was declaring then and there that His Church would be built upon that principle. They went on to conclude that it was never meant to suggest that Jesus was assigning Peter the task of actually building it. However, "The rest of the story" (which they ignored) is contained in the very next verse where Jesus also made this statement directly to Peter. It says: "<u>And</u> (Peter), I will give you the keys of the kingdom of heaven: and whatever you choose to bind on earth shall be bound in heaven: and whatever you choose to loose on earth shall be loosed in heaven." That sounds to me like Jesus intended that Peter get it done. How does one legitimately separate verse 19 from verse 18? The word "And" at the beginning of verse 19 connects them. Jesus was saying, in effect, that He would stand behind Peter as he built it.

Because Jesus' messages were the same to the Jew and Gentile alike, if we want to learn about how the Church of Jesus Christ was to be established we look to Peter for that, not Paul. Peter was the one chosen by Jesus to define both Christianity and the church, not Paul. Paul was to also teach the same Jesus-based gospel that Peter taught....period.

The entire book of Galatians, which was written by Paul, addresses the principal differences between what he (Paul) taught and what Peter taught. The book deals with the blending of those elements of "The Spirit," "Faith," "Righteous works," "Grace" and "Circumcision." The most significant differences between Paul and Peter involved the relationship between Faith, Works and Grace, with salvation at the center of it all. Peter taught the pursuit of righteousness and Paul, followed by John Calvin, more or less taught that it was a slam against The Holy Spirit to believe it possible to personally and independently perform a single righteous act. It was there in Gal. 1:6-9 that Paul spoke a curse against Peter because of the different Gospel Peter was teaching. Paul came down very hard on Peter by name. Peter rebutted Paul's doctrines merely by continuing to teach what Jesus taught. However, without calling his name, I believe the entire book of 2nd Peter was written as a rebuke against Paul and those things Paul taught which were never endorsed by Jesus.

Paul states in Galatians that when he was called "to be a minister" by Jesus' Spirit, Jesus told him that the details of the gospel which he was to preach would come to him through a continuing revelation directly from His (Jesus') Spirit. Evidently Paul did not question or attempt to compare any of what he gathered from those perceived revelations by a visit to either of the Apostles that had lived and traveled with Jesus, who would later have their own gospels written containing quotations directly from His (Jesus') lips. Perhaps he intentionally chose not to compare with them, but rather go with what he envisioned was revealed to his spirit from Jesus' Spirit. Although Jesus did not teach conflicting doctrines, there were major differences between the gospels of Matthew, Mark, Luke and John when compared to Paul's gospel,

In the fourteenth chapter of John, Jesus said this to His Apostles: *"But the Comforter, which is the Holy Ghost, whom the Father will send in my name, he shall teach you all things, and bring all things to your remembrance, whatsoever I have said unto you."* Evidently the Spirit that visited Paul did not think it necessary to teach him the same things that He (The

Spirit) had taught everyone else and we must ask ourselves why the Holy Spirit would be putting out different conflicting teachings to different people. If we agree here that The Spirit of Jesus or The Spirit of God would not teach contradictory gospels, then that would lead us to conclude that some of what Paul taught was from his own imagination and is a perfect illustration of just how powerful a perceived spiritual connection to Jesus can be, whether it is legitimate or (in Paul's case) at least partly imagined. That not only applies to Paul but to all of us as well.

If we look objectively at the "Rock" that Paul built his church on, it would surely lead some of us to conclude that the rock is a rock named "Paul."

Although Peter was Bishop of the Church at Rome and is claimed by The Roman Catholic Church to be that church's beginning, apparently the large, complicated and supreme bureaucracy that evolved to rule The Roman Catholic Church and establish its elaborate ceremonial system was all put in place well after Peter's death because that is not what Peter taught. He taught the opposite.

Peter's writings concerning the details of the Church and Christianity are the same as Jesus taught and are contained in 1st Peter 1, 2, 3, 4 & 5 and 2nd Peter 1, 2 & 3. There's not a lot of reading there and it speaks for itself. So, if anyone wants to know about Jesus' definition of Christianity, read all about it in Peter's writings. Unlike Paul, Peter didn't deviate from what Jesus had taught:

- Peter taught in unambiguous terms that the word of God (The original Bible) is alive and well without contradiction by The Holy Spirit (as did Paul) and is the only source for Christianity.

  1st Pet. 1: 23 & 25 "Being born again, not of corruptible seed, but of incorruptible, <u>by the word of God</u>, which liveth and abideth for ever… And this is the word which by the gospel is preached unto you."

- Peter emphasized repentance as part of the process of following Jesus:

  "The Lord is not slack concerning his promise, as some men count slackness; but is longsuffering toward us, not willing that any should perish, but that all should come to repentance." (2nd Peter 2:9)

- Interestingly, this is what Peter taught about church leadership in 1st Peter, 5th Chapter:

  "The elders which are among you I exhort, who am also an elder, and a witness of the sufferings of Christ, and also a partaker of the glory that shall be revealed:² Feed the flock of God which is among you, taking the oversight thereof, not by constraint, but willingly; not for filthy lucre, but of a ready mind;³ Neither as being lords over God's heritage, but being examples to the flock."

- Peter's teachings do not support the kind of "relationship" between God and mankind that is currently being promoted by many churches. This is what Peter said about it in 1st Peter 1:14-17:

"As obedient children, not fashioning yourselves according to the former lusts in your ignorance: But as he which hath called you is holy, so be ye holy in all manner of conversation; Because it is written, Be ye holy; for I am holy. And if ye call on the Father, who without respect of persons judgeth according to every man's work, pass the time of your sojourning here in fear."

• Peter also taught throughout his writings in 1st and 2nd Peter that we have personal responsibility to learn about and seek after God's righteousness and strongly insinuates that we do not become righteous merely by believing about Jesus. I won't reproduce the many quotes about it here. It will make an interesting read for those who have that interest.

• Peter, like Jesus, had very little to say about praying. He did not say that God required or expected it of us nor did he attempt to establish it as a ritual as did Paul. (No, I don't have anything against praying.... as Jesus taught.)

What I have documented about Paul's influence on the definition and practice of Christianity is self evident and is quite different than what Peter and Jesus taught. The information I have presented creates a unique dilemma because, as serious as the contradictions are between Paul and Peter and Jesus, practically no one wants to talk about them and some may deny they exist even after reading this accounting of them.

It, of course, is inappropriate to question either the sincerity or the legitimacy of anyone's perceived relationship with Jesus. That doesn't change the fact that there are many people who are unaware that the origins of their own beliefs and practices were not taught nor supported by Jesus. Some accept whatever they have been taught about God and Jesus without question. Consequently, their perceived relationship with Jesus is based on those teachings by Paul that contradicted what Jesus taught. It gets complicated. Some will say to you without blinking an eye: "I don't care what the Bible says; I know what I've been taught." How does that work? In the evolution of any relationship, they sometimes just naturally change as we learn new and significant information about the party with whom we have the relationship. So it is in a relationship with Jesus.

This study challenges many of Paul's questionable doctrines knowing full well that most of us don't want to contend with the issues that would accompany any changing of them. We don't want to start all over again in our basic concepts about Jesus and God and our spiritual relationships with them; also, we don't want to admit we have been misled to the extent we have been. After all, how is it possible that our own spirit could have been so deceived? Could it be that we get our emotions confused with our spirit? When it comes to something as important as "God," we would like to think we are not so easily manipulated: "I might be misled to buy 'a bill of goods' for something like an automobile or a stock or even be taken-in by a politician, but I could never be bamboozled about 'God;'" Really?

On the other hand, if any agree that what is presented here from scripture leads to a different and more logical conclusion than what we have been taught, why would it now be wrong, without any fanfare, to actually start giving priority to Jesus' teachings from this point forward and discard that bamboozled baggage? We are not required to declare anything to any person or to any organization and it doesn't mean we are denying Jesus just because we don't follow their rules accompanying individual church "membership." They would have us believe that we are in fact denying Him unless we do exactly as they say. It's not up to them to decide how that works. We don't have to go before a tribunal or make a public confession or profession or any of that stuff. We don't have to go to a single person and confess that we have followed after Paul and not Jesus. Besides that, they may think we're nuts. The objective is to always be on the "same page" with Jesus; so, just do it independently and it will enhance that personal relationship to a new level. Remember the simple rules: "Love God" and "Do unto others as you would have them do unto you."

So, after knowing without question that Paul contradicts Jesus in some of his fundamental teachings, why is it that we still gravitate toward Paul while calling ourselves Christians? Here's an obvious theory that probably nails it: First of all that is what we are taught; but even more precisely, Jesus declared that He came into the world to call us to righteousness and according to scripture that's also what He told Paul to do. Paul, on the other hand, gave us an excuse not to pursue righteousness when he declared himself to be a "wretched" man, not able to attain any righteousness. So we are taught by Paul to lean heavily on God's grace while believing God sees us as having the righteousness of Jesus even if we never perform a single righteous act. Therefore, Jesus becomes our symbol while Paul becomes our pattern. Paul pretty much insinuated that Jesus died as a guarantee that we can ignore God's standards and live out our life in any manner we choose and when we die, still go to heaven. While the "Paul people" will never officially endorse that statement, it is nevertheless what they practice and is contrary to what Jesus taught.

All of Paul's writings collectively become "The Gospel of Paul" and Paul's gospel has been given preference by many over Matthew's or Mark's or Luke's or John's. Paul's doctrines are presented daily in familiar sounding sermons around the world. They are also imbedded in many so-called Christian songs that we sing and learn from without giving any thought to their origin. Many of those great sounding old songs are still in my mind and reside there as in reverence to the single focus of my earlier teachings and thoughts toward Jesus. They taught us to sing: "*What can wash away my sins; nothing but the blood of Jesus....What can make me whole again; nothing but the blood of Jesus. Oh precious is the flow that makes me white as snow. No other fount I know; nothing but the* blood of Jesus." Also there is: "Jesus paid it all. All to Him I owe. Sin had left a crimson stain. He washed it white as snow." Then there is: "Are you washed in the blood....In the soul-cleansing blood of the lamb?" Do you remember: "Would you be free from your burden of sin? There's power in the blood, power in the blood." And finally the ending of the song "Just as I am" summarizes the "blood doctrine" well: "To Thee whose blood can cleanse each spot, oh Lamb of God I come....I come."

When many of those "Paul people" sing: "Would you be free from your passion and pride... There's power in the blood, power in the blood," they don't really expect to actually change anything in their lives, especially their passion or their pride. They see it (like Paul) as they're now having no more responsibility for it. That's where they get their freedom. That is their freedom. Jesus died for that?

Paul made statements that are not found anywhere else in the Bible which were latched onto and established as Church doctrine taught both by teaching and by song. Another example of Paul's teaching that is reflected in several songs is found in Ephesians 1:14 where Paul wrote: "Which is the earnest of our inheritance until the redemption of the purchased possession, unto the praise of his glory." Paul is the only person who ever said that. He concluded here (and other places) that God allowed Jesus to die in order for His death to become the focus of our redemption and that God did, in fact, purchase us by and through His death. Although Jesus did say that His death was a "Ransom for many," He did not say we were to be redeemed only by the death itself. He specifically told us how that works and it was not dependant on His death: *"Why call ye me Lord, Lord and do not the things which I say"* (Luke 6:46). Paul's use of the word "purchased" emerged in a song you may remember which reads, in part: *"Purchasing my pardon on Calvary's tree."* Paul is the only Bible character who ever said that. Jesus never said it. God never said it through Moses or any of the Prophets and is just another example of Paul's guiding the congregations around repentance and the pursuit of righteousness towards the miraculous workings of the Holy Spirit (as Paul defined it).

Another popular and beautiful old song that reflects what Paul taught is "I will sing of my Redeemer." Songs are powerful emotional tools to instill doctrine in the congregations and this song contains as much doctrine as any I have heard. The following is quoted from the song:

> *"I will sing of my Redeemer*
> *And His wondrous love to me*
> *On the cruel cross He suffered*
> *From the curse to set me free*
>
> *Sing oh sing of my Redeemer*
> *With His blood He purchased me*
> *On the cross He sealed my pardon*
> *Paid the debt and made me free."*

That is a beautiful sounding old song that summarizes a salvation without repentance and without learning about and pursuing God's standards. I never considered the implication of just what the song was teaching when I was singing it or that it completely contradicts the following teaching from Jesus:

> "*Then said Jesus to those Jews which believed on Him: "If ye continue in My word, then are ye My disciples indeed; and ye shall know the truth, and **the truth shall make you free**....If the Son therefore shall make you free, ye shall be free indeed." John 8:31-32 & 36.*

The song teaches that Jesus died as payment to purchase us and make us free. Jesus said we should learn about and follow His teachings because therein lies the real truth to make us free. According to Paul "Jesus paid it all" when He died. As important as the matter is, why would Jesus not have taught it the same as Paul did in a straightforward and unambiguous way? Not only did He not teach it, He taught the very opposite.

None of that or anything else I have written here is intended to minimize the sacrificial nature of the death of Jesus. On the contrary, nothing in either of those songs supported what Jesus declared His mission to be. The shedding of Jesus' blood being the direct result of His mission is just as deserving of our praise as if it were the finished work of salvation. Just because Jesus told His disciples to remember Him and what He was about to die for did not suggest that His death was to be a substitute for repentance or for choosing to learn about and attempt to pattern after God's righteousness. According to Jesus, He was born for the single purpose of teaching us about those two things. He was eventually killed because that was what He was teaching to the crowds and it threatened to come between the people and the religious leaders of that day. His blood was shed for many for the remission of sins because they had Him killed to silence Him from carrying out His mission. Even so, many focus on His death as the primary source of their "Christian" faith and experience. We are indeed saved as a result of the shedding of the wonderful and precious blood of Jesus. It is unfortunate that it is also being taught that the shedding of his blood cancelled what He had taught earlier about repentance and the pursuit of righteousness.

Many other Christian songs are designed to present "salvation" as consisting only of our acknowledgment that Jesus' martyrdom was designed by God to bring us into reconciliation with Him. The words of a beautifully written song is a powerful tool that is used to plant their presentation of the God image they chose to install in the minds of their congregations and music has been given an increasingly larger role in canned worship performances.

I can still hum most of those good ole songs with as much respect and gratitude to Jesus as ever; but I do it now with what I believe is a better understanding of just what they mean, or don't mean. His spilled blood and death should forever be revered as a precious price that He paid to bring us the "simple" message of salvation and without it being seen as a substitute for repentance and the pursuit of God's righteousness (Be ye holy for I am holy). That is a good example of why we should always follow Jesus when His teachings conflict with Paul. We can adjust from those conflicting teachings by Paul to a

Jesus based foundation without trashing the melody of those great old songs that linger in our memories. A little tweaking here and there in our understanding and we've got it right.

Being fully saturated and indoctrinated in what Paul taught and turning our back on what Jesus taught, it is difficult for many of us to now consider "Christianity" in any other light except as Paul taught it. I suspect there are some who believe they've just got too much invested in Paul to now switch over to Jesus and I am aware that this presentation of Paul's teachings comparing them to Jesus' teachings creates a serious affront to traditional Christianity as it has been taught and practiced by many. Jesus said that some will believe and some will not believe. So be it.

I still think of Jesus' crucifixion with as much emotion and regret as ever because His death is just as worthy of our praise if only because of His dedication to His mission. Yes, He did come to save us from sin but I no longer believe He died just so the rest of the world can "play-like" we're good or righteous when we're not. How could that ever "*turn them from darkness to light, and from the power of Satan unto God?*" It couldn't! Still, I respect any differences of opinion from my own. Been there....done that! This would be a great subject for discussion in a fair and open forum but The Church Institution will never allow that to happen within their territory and jurisdiction. Just as in the larger political environment, a large percentage of their membership is biblically illiterate and they want to keep it that way.

One difficult barrier to approaching, understanding, and dealing with "The Paul Factor" is the declaration by some, like the late W.A. Criswell, that the Bible is to be viewed as being totally, completely and absolutely…word by word… inerrant. The Bible is a wonderful collection of writings by many people who declared they were inspired by God to write what they wrote. However, to declare that it has no conflicting statements is to paint oneself into a corner. That is one reason we got off-track when we were led away from Jesus' teachings toward Paul's teachings. They narrowly pointed to what they wanted us to read and told us how to think and we were not willing to compare the differences existing in the total text and go on to acknowledge that…yes, there is indeed contradiction easily observed just by comparing Jesus' teachings with Paul's teachings. I believe one of the principle reasons clergy in general are now turning away from scripture is because it is becoming more and more difficult to explain their historic fixed doctrines to an increasingly knowledgeable congregation. In order to deal with those issues, many now attempt to trash scripture and rely more on "emotion" as being the cradle of their new "millennium gospel." The matter becomes even more confusing because while some officially declare the bible to be totally inerrant, others deny scripture's relevance altogether, yet both positions promote the gospel of Paul as being the fundamental Christian theme. They have, in fact, collectively created the perfect religious storm which they're all trying hard to ignore. The book <u>Surprised by Hope</u> by N T Wright is a perfect example of the inconsistency existing in Christian doctrine. It is an eloquently written adoption of the gospel of Paul and it specifically denies any authority of scripture. The difference between Criswell and

Wright is a 180 degree swing of the pendulum. Has anyone become dizzy trying to follow that swing?

The few watering wells we were led to drink from in the Bible were man-made wells and if consolidated, could all be contained on two or three pages in a book having a thousand pages. We, as sheep, are led blindfolded to their feed troughs and then turned out to pasture in fields having no grass. While most clergy admonish us to read the bible, the "Bible Study" materials they give us are narrowly designed to reinforce what they have already taught us and it appears we never venture beyond the principal doctrines they would have us hold to. I suspect that some of them do not believe we can connect the dots. There is no doubt that many of them have not themselves connected the dots, or rather ignored them. If taken at face value, there are conflicting statements throughout scripture in spite of how they were explained-away in Bible-Seminaries and from behind pulpits. That in itself does not diminish or devalue the worthiness of scripture. It did not have to be recreated by zealous evangelists in order to enhance its value. It stands alone and complete without their tinkering.

The contradictions contained in Paul's teachings have been available for all to read since the printing press was invented in 1450. That was 554 years ago and underscores the impact the promotion of Paul's perceived spiritualization has had over the written word. Jesus said: "God is a Spirit;" and according to scripture there should be no confusion between God's Spirit and God's Word. It was Paul that first created that confusion and the comparisons between Jesus and Paul I have used here speak for themselves. Paul may have taught what he taught for the same reason it is still being taught today. It's harder to "draw a crowd" when you're teaching them to learn about and seriously attempt to follow the righteousness of God.

Paul's whole concept of "Church" gave power to the Institution and when the reformers broke from the Roman Catholic Church, Paul's teachings followed them with the same authority and power over the congregations. The principle thing they reformed was who was to be in charge of the congregations and who got to take the money to the bank.

The "Great Commission" that Jesus gave to disciples who followed Him was "Go ye therefore and teach all people to observe all those things that I have commanded you;" (paraphrased) and those Teachings of Jesus (not Paul) were to be the foundational concepts of His church. Peter taught it just as Jesus taught it; Paul taught part of it to legitimize the other part that he made up. There have been many dedicated people who accepted Jesus' commission and went to distant lands to "teach all people" around the world. Some sacrificed greatly, some suffered and some even died, only to spread Paul's gospel while mistaking it to be the gospel of Jesus Christ.

Today's presentations of Christianity as well as other religions reflect the scientific summary of everything that has been learned about human nature and how to change and mould people to accomplish a desired outcome. The "hucksters" that pull the strings just to jerk us around have a natural ready-made market just waiting to be devoured. It consists of 7 billion people staring into space with many of them wondering: "What the hell am I doing here?" Human nature is the same today as it was 2,000 years ago and the "church's" scientifically designed thesis had its origin with the "Apostle" Paul… way back then.

In further contradiction to Paul, Jesus once said in Mat. 9:13-14:

"They that are whole need not a physician, but they that are sick. But go ye and learn what that means, I will have mercy, and not sacrifice: for I am not come to call the righteous, but sinners to repentance."

Paul, on the other hand, rarely conceded that any righteousness could ever exist in anyone at any time. That teaching by Jesus did not meet his agenda. To summarize Paul's clandestine doctrine: We are to feel guilt if only by experiencing those common human instincts which are natural to all mankind. It doesn't matter that we don't act-out all of our feelings about such things as anger or lust, Paul would still give us no credit for that, nor did John Calvin. They both assigned guilt to a natural impulse alone and struggled to make good people believe they were totally bad. They also went on to teach us (by insinuation) that we individually and personally carry a responsibility for Jesus' death creating an obligation to "join" their Christian movement for that sake alone. Consequently, many times a person's so-called "conversion," evolving out of a "Paulinian" guilt-trip, is directed to false premises. Today's clergy who now lead us down that Paul path to "conversion" go on to assume the role of "Dr. Feelgood," furnishing us an environment to confess to it all while being blessed only by our presence there. We, of course, pay them to do all of that although little or none of it represents the church of Jesus Christ. We tolerate a lot of stuff in our "play-like" approach to Christianity only because it enables us to turn our back on what Jesus taught: "Do unto others as you would have them do unto you."

One can legitimately ask: "What's left of Christianity without those teachings of Paul that you would trash?" Well, for starters we've got the same God that created the universe and every living thing in it, including man. We've got the same Jesus, the Son of God, who was sent by God to teach us about God's righteousness and to demonstrate that righteousness to us. We've still got all of the same promises that God and Jesus made to us, including an abundant life both here and after our death. The primary change would be to learn about and personally apply the simplification of what Jesus taught rather than the highly complicated ceremonial-bureaucratic-religiosity having its beginning with Paul and designed to create personal guilt in the congregations and/or surrendered allegiance to the church institution and its programs. When a church institution fails to promote the God of the bible that institution has itself become the god they promote.

So, what should one be called who is a follower of Paul, a "Paulite" or what? You don't think that sounds right? You say you've never heard of a "Paulite?" Me either. How about a "Paulinian;" ever hear them called by that name? Me either. Perhaps a "Paul person" is more appropriate. Whatever name it is they are to be called is a name that represents one of the world's largest un-named religious groups who, while thinking themselves to be "Christians" are rather (according to scripture) more followers of Paul than followers of Jesus Christ.

Jesus said: *"For verily I say unto you, that many prophets and righteous men have desired to see those things which ye see, and have not seen them; and to hear those things which ye hear, and have not heard them." (Mat. 13:7)*

Once seen and heard they cannot be ignored. How different would the Christian world be today if people were actually followers of Jesus and his teachings?

None of what is written here denies that Paul taught many wonderfully expressed truths that line-up with the balance of scripture. What we have also presented describes other significant things that he taught which either was not taught by Jesus or directly contradicted Jesus and cannot be allowed to stand alone. Paul was not given authority over Jesus and his independent teachings deserve to be judged directly by what Jesus taught and died for. Those contradictory teachings by Paul are imbedded alongside many other teachings of bible-based truth; yet, as it actually happened, it was mostly those contradictions to Jesus which have been extracted by "Christian" theologians and were used as the foundation for most "Christian" doctrine as the church was established and promoted. That had the effect of putting the institution of the church and its leadership in charge of the congregations while turning Jesus into an honorary "Religious Icon," deserving of our praise and worship and love, yet without any authority except as each person sensed and determined it within their individual mind and spirit. That resulted in little uniformity in Jesus' image to the congregation. Jesus became just whoever and whatever each person wanted Him to be. Eventually, they (Paul's independent teachings) were given priority over most everything Jesus had taught. I know, it's weird; but the writings speak for themselves. If you are ready to close the book on this and you still question this challenge to Paul's writings, don't just brush it all off without first thoughtfully comparing them once again using only the KJV version in order to observe and understand the differences between Paul's and Jesus' teachings. After all, we are seeking the truth here and are willing to tear down walls and old taboos to find it.

Thanks for taking the time to read this book. Whether or not you agree with anything that has been said or concluded, you'll have to admit it's interesting; perhaps interesting enough not to forget.